1961

C000146142

The KINGS TREASURIES
OF LITERATURE

GENERAL EDITOR
SIR A·T· QUILLER COUCH

LONDON : J·M·DENT & SONS LTD.

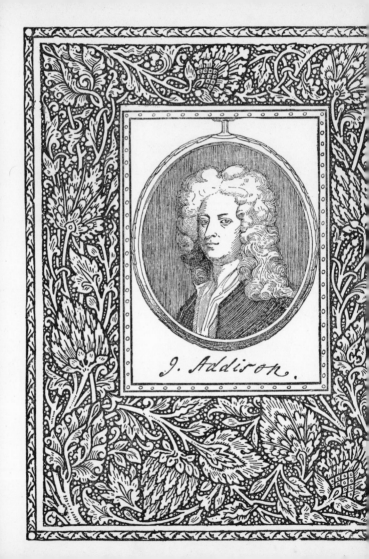

J. Addison.

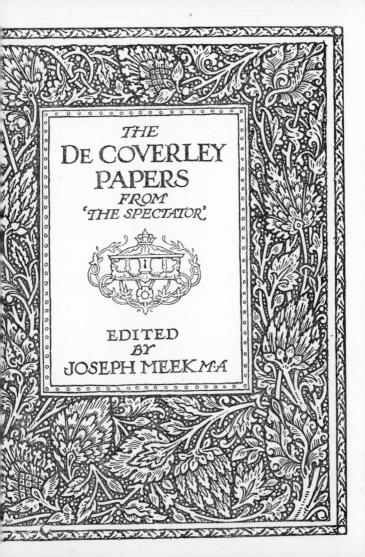

THE
DE COVERLEY
PAPERS
FROM
'THE SPECTATOR'

EDITED
BY
JOSEPH MEEK M·A

All rights reserved
Made in Great Britain
at the
Aldine Press · Letchworth · Herts
for
J. M. DENT & SONS LTD
Aldine House · Bedford Street · London
First published in this edition 1920
Last reprinted 1961

INTRODUCTION

No character in our literature, not even Mr. Pickwick, has more endeared himself to successive generations of readers than Addison's Sir Roger de Coverley: there are many figures in drama and fiction of whom we feel that they are in a way personal friends of our own, that once introduced to us they remain a permanent part of our little world. It is the abiding glory of Dickens, it is one of Shakespeare's abiding glories, to have created many such: but we look to find these characters in the novel or the play: the essay by virtue of its limitations of space is unsuited for character-studies, and even in the subject of our present reading the difficulty of hunting the various Coverley Essays down in the great number of *Spectator* Papers is some small drawback. But here before the birth of the modern English novel we have a full-length portrait of such a character as we have described, in addition to a number of other more sketchy but still convincing delineations of English types. We are brought into the society of a fine old-fashioned country gentleman, simple, generous, and upright, with just those touches of whimsicality and those lovable faults which go straight to our hearts: and all so charmingly described that these Essays have delighted all who have read them since they first began to appear on the breakfast-tables of the polite world in Queen Anne's day.

" Addison's " Sir Roger we have called him, and be sure that honest Dick Steele, even if he drew the first outlines of the figure, would not bear us a grudge for so doing. Whoever first thought of Sir Roger, and however many little touches may have been added by other hands, he remains Addison's creation: and furthermore it does not matter a snap of the fingers whether any actual person served as the model from which the picture was taken. Of all the bootless quests that literary criticism can under-take, this search for " the original " is the least valuable. The artist's mind is a crucible which transmutes and re-creates: to vary the metaphor, the marble springs to life under the workman's hands: we can almost see it happening in these Essays: and we know how often enough a writer finds his own creation kicking over the traces, as it were, and becoming almost independent of his volition. There is no original for Sir Roger or Falstaff or Mr. Micawber: they may not have sprung Athena-like fully armed out of the author's head, and they may have been suggested by some one he had in mind. But once created they came into a full-blooded life with personalities entirely of their own.

A vastly more useful quest, one in fact of absorbing interest, is the attempt to follow the artist's method, to trace the devices which he adopts to bring to our notice all those various traits by which we judge of character. The prose writer has this much advantage over the playwright, that he can represent his *dramatis personæ* in a greater number of different situations, and furthermore can criticise them and draw our special attention to what he wishes to have stressed: he can even say that such and such thoughts and motives are in their minds. Not so the dramatist: his space is limited and he is cribbed, cabined, and confined by having to give a convincing imitation of real life, where we cannot tell what is going on in the minds of even our most intimate friends. Thus the audience is often left uncertain of the purport of what it sees and hears: the ugly and inartistic convention of the aside must be used very sparingly if the play is to ring true; and so it is that we shall find voluminous discussions on the subject, for instance, of how Shakespeare meant such and such a character to be interpreted. It stands to reason that the character in fiction can to this same extent be more artificial. It is a test of the self-control and artistic restraint of the novelist if he can refrain from diving too deep into the unknown and arrogating to himself an impossibly full knowledge of the mental processes of other people. And now notice how Addison gives us just such revelations of the old Knight's character as the observant spectator would gather from friendly intercourse with him. We see Sir Roger at home, ruling his household and the village with a genial if somewhat autocratic sway: we see him in London, taking the cicerone who pilots him round Westminster Abbey for a monument of wit and learning: and so on and so forth. There is no need to catalogue these occasions: what we have said should suffice to point out a very fruitful line of study which may help the reader to a full appreciation of Addison's work. "Good wine needs no bush," and the Coverley Essays are good wine if ever there was such.

The study of the style is also of the greatest value. Addison lived at a time when our modern English prose had recently found itself. We admire the splendour of the Miltonic style, and lose ourselves in the rich harmonies of Sir Thomas Browne's work; but after all prose is needed for ordinary every-day jog-trot purposes and must be clear and straightforward. It can still remain a very attractive instrument of speech or writing, and in Addison's hands it fulfilled to perfection the needs of the essay style. He avoids verbiage and excessive adornment, he is content to tell what he sees or knows or thinks as simply as possible (and even with a tendency towards the conversational), and he has an inimitable feeling for just the right word, just the most elegantly turned phrase and period. Do not imagine this sort of thing is the result of a mere gift for style: true, it could not happen without that, but neither can it happen without a great deal of careful thought, a scrupulous choice, and balancing of word against word, phrase against phrase. Because all this is done and because the result is so clear and runs so smoothly, it requires an effort on our part to realise the great amount of work involved: *Ars est celare artem*: and in such an essay as that describing the picture gallery in Sir Roger's house we can see the pictures in front of our eyes precisely because the description is so clear-cut, so free from unnecessary decoration, and yet so picturesque and attractive.

A very short acquaintance will enable the reader to appreciate Addison's charming humour and sane grasp of character. The high moral tone of his work, the common-sense and broad culture and literary insight which caused the *Spectator* to exert a profound influence over a dissolute age, these can only be seen by a more extended reading of the Essays, and those who are interested cannot do better than obtain some general selection such as that of Arnold.

Biographical and historical details are somewhat outside the scope of the present Essay. A short Chronological Table is appended, and the reader cannot be too strongly recommended to study Johnson's Life of Addison, which is one of the best of the Lives of the Poets, and in which the literary criticism is in Johnson's best vein. And Thackeray's *Esmond* contains some delightful passages introducing Richard Steele and his entourage, with an interesting scene in Addison's lodgings. It is perhaps as well to mention that the *Spectator* grew out of Addison's collaboration with Steele in a similar periodical entitled the *Tatler*. There were several writers besides these two concerned in the *Spectator*, notably Budgell. (The letters at the end of most of the papers are signatures: C., L., I. and O. are the marks of Addison's work, R. and T. of Steele's, and X. of Budgell's.) We have stories of Addison's resentment of their tampering with his favourite character; it is even said that he killed the Knight

*

off in his annoyance at one paper which represented him in an unfitting situation. We cannot judge of the truth of such stories. In any case it was Addison who controlled the whole tenor and policy of the paper, wisely steering as clear as possible of politics, and thereby broadening his appeal and reaching a wider public, and it was Addison's kindly and mellow criticism of life that informed the whole work. His remaining literary productions, popular at the time, have receded into the background: but the *Spectator* will keep his name alive as long as English literature survives.

(In this selection only those essays have been chosen which bear directly on Sir Roger or the *Spectator* Club: several have been omitted which refer to him only *en passant* or as a peg on which to hang some disquisition, and also one other which is wholly out of keeping with Sir Roger's character.)

CHRONOLOGICAL TABLE

1672. Birth of Addison and Steele.
1697. Addison elected Fellow of Magdalen College, Oxford.
1701, 3, 5, 22. Steele's Plays.
1702. Accession of Queen Anne.
1704. Addison's *Campaign* (poem celebrating Blenheim).
1706. Addison's *Rosamond* (opera).
1709–11. Steele's *Tatler*.
1711–12–14. The *Spectator*.
1713. Addison's *Cato* (play).
1714. Accession of George I.
1717. Addison appointed Secretary of State.
1719. Death of Addison.
1729. Death of Steele.

THE DE COVERLEY PAPERS

No. 1.   THURSDAY, MARCH 1, 1710–11

Non fumum ex fulgore, sed ex fumo dare lucem
Cogitat, ut speciosa dehinc miracula promat.

HOR. Ars Poet. ver. 143.

One with a flash begins, and ends in smoke;
The other out of smoke brings glorious light,
And (without raising expectation high)
Surprises us with dazzling miracles.

ROSCOMMON.

I HAVE observed, that a reader seldom peruses a book
with pleasure, until he knows whether the writer of
it be a black or a fair man, of a mild or choleric disposition, married or a bachelor, with other particulars of the like nature, that conduce very much to
the right understanding of an author.   To gratify
this curiosity, which is so natural to a reader, I
design this paper and my next as prefatory discourses
to my following writings, and shall give some account
in them of the several persons that are engaged
in this work.   As the chief trouble of compiling,
digesting, and correcting will fall to my share, I
must do myself the justice to open the work with
my own history.

Black. Dark.   Choleric. Liable to anger.
Digesting. Arranging methodically.

I was born to a small hereditary estate, which, according to the tradition of the village where it lies, was bounded by the same hedges and ditches in William the Conqueror's time that it is at present, and has been delivered down from father to son whole and entire, without the loss or acquisition of a single field or meadow, during the space of six hundred years. There runs a story in the family, that before my birth my mother dreamt that she was brought to bed of a judge: whether this might proceed from a lawsuit which was then depending in the family, or my father's being a justice of the peace, I cannot determine; for I am not so vain as to think it presaged any dignity that I should arrive at in my future life, though that was the interpretation which the neighbourhood put upon it. The gravity of my behaviour at my very first appearance in the world, and all the time that I sucked, seemed to favour my mother's dream: for, as she has often told me, I threw away my rattle before I was two months old, and would not make use of my coral until they had taken away the bells from it.

As for the rest of my infancy, there being nothing in it remarkable, I shall pass it over in silence. I find, that, during my nonage, I had the reputation of a very sullen youth, but was always a favourite of my schoolmaster, who used to say, that my parts were solid, and would wear well. I had not been long

Depending. Modern English *pending.*
Nonage. Minority.   *Parts.* Powers.

at the University, before I distinguished myself by a most profound silence; for during the space of eight years, excepting in the public exercises of the college, I scarce uttered the quantity of an hundred words; and indeed do not remember that I ever spoke three sentences together in my whole life. Whilst I was in this learned body, I applied myself with so much diligence to my studies, that there are very few celebrated books, either in the learned or the modern tongues, which I am not acquainted with.

Upon the death of my father, I was resolved to travel into foreign countries, and therefore left the University, with the character of an odd unaccountable fellow, that had a great deal of learning, if I would but show it. An insatiable thirst after knowledge carried me into all the countries of Europe, in which there was anything new or strange to be seen; nay, to such a degree was my curiosity raised, that having read the controversies of some great men concerning the antiquities of Egypt, I made a voyage to Grand Cairo, on purpose to take the measure of a pyramid : and, as soon as I had set myself right in that particular, returned to my native country with great satisfaction.

I have passed my latter years in this city, where I am frequently seen in most public places, though there are not above half a dozen of my select friends that know me; of whom my next paper shall give

---

Public exercises. Examinations for degrees at Oxford and Cambridge formerly took the form of public debates.

a more particular account. There is no place of general resort, wherein I do not often make my appearance; sometimes I am seen thrusting my head into a round of politicians at Will's, and listening with great attention to the narratives that are made in those little circular audiences. Sometimes I smoke a pipe at Child's, and, whilst I seem attentive to nothing but the *Postman*, overhear the conversation of every table in the room. I appear on Sunday nights at St. James's coffee-house, and sometimes join the little committee of politics in the inner room, as one who comes there to hear and improve. My face is likewise very well known at the Grecian, the Cocoa-Tree, and in the theatres both of Drury Lane and the Hay-Market. I have been taken for a merchant upon the Exchange for above these ten years, and sometimes pass for a Jew in the assembly of stock-jobbers at Jonathan's: in short, wherever I see a cluster of people, I always mix with them, though I never open my lips but in my own club.

Thus I live in the world rather as a spectator of mankind, than as one of the species, by which means I have made myself a speculative statesman, soldier, merchant, and artisan, without ever meddling with any practical part in life. I am very well versed in the theory of a husband or a father, and can

Will's, Child's, St. James's, Grecian. Coffee-houses; all these, and the cocoa-houses too, tended to become the special haunts of members of some particular party, profession, etc.; *e.g.*, Will's was literary, St. James's Whig.

Postman. A weekly newspaper.

discern the errors in the economy, business, and diversion of others, better than those who are engaged in them; as standers-by discover blots, which are apt to escape those who are in the game. I never espoused any party with violence, and am resolved to observe an exact neutrality between the Whigs and Tories, unless I shall be forced to declare myself by the hostilities of either side. In short, I have acted in all the parts of my life as a looker-on, which is the character I intend to preserve in this paper.

I have given the reader just so much of my history and character, as to let him see I am not altogether unqualified for the business I have undertaken. As for other particulars in my life and adventures, I shall insert them in following papers, as I shall see occasion. In the meantime, when I consider how much I have seen, read, and heard, I begin to blame my own taciturnity; and, since I have neither time nor inclination to communicate the fulness of my heart in speech, I am resolved to do it in writing, and to print myself out, if possible, before I die. I have been often told by my friends, that it is pity so many useful discoveries which I have made should be in the possession of a silent man. For this reason, therefore, I shall publish a sheet-full of thoughts every morning, for the benefit of my contemporaries; and if I can any way contribute to the diversion or improvement of the country in which I live, I shall leave it, when I am

Economy. Household management.
Blots. Exposed pieces in backgammon.

summoned out of it, with the secret satisfaction of
thinking that I have not lived in vain.

There are three very material points which I have
not spoken to in this paper; and which, for several
important reasons, I must keep to myself, at least
for some time: I mean, an account of my name,
my age, and my lodgings. I must confess, I would
gratify my reader in anything that is reasonable;
but as for these three particulars, though I am
sensible they might tend very much to the embellish-
ment of my paper, I cannot yet come to a resolution
of communicating them to the public. They would
indeed draw me out of that obscurity which I have
enjoyed for many years, and expose me in public
places to several salutes and civilities, which have
been always very disagreeable to me; for the greatest
pain I can suffer, is the being talked to, and being
stared at. It is for this reason likewise, that I keep
my complexion and dress as very great secrets;
though it is not impossible, but I may make discoveries of both in the progress of the work I have
undertaken.

After having been thus particular upon myself,
I shall, in to-morrow's paper, give an account of
those gentlemen who are concerned with me in this
work; for, as I have before intimated, a plan of it
is laid and concerted (as all other matters of im-
portance are) in a club. However, as my friends
have engaged me to stand in the front, those who

Spoken to. Referred to.   *Complexion.* Countenance.
          Discoveries. Disclosures.

have a mind to correspond with me, may direct their letters to the *Spectator*, at Mr. Buckley's in Little Britain. For I must further acquaint the reader, that, though our club meets only on Tuesdays and Thursdays, we have appointed a committee to sit every night, for the inspection of all such papers as may contribute to the advancement of the public weal.   C.

No. 2.   FRIDAY, MARCH 2

Ast alii sex
Et plures uno conclamant ore.
                                    JUV. *Sat.* vii. ver. 167.
Six more at least join their consenting voice.

THE first of our society is a gentleman of Worcestershire, of ancient descent, a baronet, his name is Sir Roger de Coverley. His great-grandfather was inventor of that famous country-dance which is called after him. All who know that shire are very well acquainted with the parts and merits of Sir Roger. He is a gentleman that is very singular in his behaviour, but his singularities proceed from his good sense, and are contradictions to the manners of the world, only as he thinks the world is in the wrong. However this humour creates him no enemies, for he does nothing with sourness or obstinacy; and his being unconfined to modes and forms, makes him but the readier and more capable to please and oblige all who know him. When he is in town, he lives in Soho Square. It is said, he keeps himself a bachelor by reason he was crossed in love by

a perverse beautiful widow of the next county to
him.   Before this disappointment, Sir Roger was
what you call a Fine Gentleman, had often supped
with my Lord Rochester and Sir George Etherege,
fought a duel upon his first coming to town, and
kicked Bully Dawson in a public coffee-house for
calling him youngster.   But being ill-used by the
above-mentioned widow, he was very serious for
a year and a half; and though, his temper being
naturally jovial, he at last got over it, he grew care-
less of himself, and never dressed afterwards.   He
continues to wear a coat and doublet of the same
cut that were in fashion at the time of his repulse,
which, in his merry humours, he tells us, has been
in and out twelve times since he first wore it.   He
is now in his fifty-sixth year, cheerful, gay, and
hearty; keeps a good house both in town and
country;   a great lover of mankind;   but there
is such a mirthful cast in his behaviour, that he is
rather beloved than esteemed.   His tenants grow
rich, his servants look satisfied, all the young women
profess love to him, and the young men are glad of
his company: when he comes into a house he calls
the servants by their names, and talks all the way
upstairs to a visit.   I must not omit, that Sir Roger
is a justice of the Quorum; that he fills the chair
at a quarter-session with great abilities, and three

Lord Rochester and Sir George Etherege. Well-known leaders
of fashion and dissipation.
Bully Dawson. A notorious swaggerer and sharper.
Dressed. I.e., fashionably.
Quorum. Panel of magistrates.

months ago gained universal applause by explaining a passage in the Game Act.

The gentleman next in esteem and authority among us, is another bachelor, who is a member of the Inner Temple; a man of great probity, wit, and understanding; but he has chosen his place of residence rather to obey the direction of an old humoursome father, than in pursuit of his own inclinations. He was placed there to study the laws of the land, and is the most learned of any of the house in those of the stage. Aristotle and Longinus are much better understood by him than Littleton or Coke. The father sends up every post questions relating to marriage-articles, leases, and tenures, in the neighbourhood; all which questions he agrees with an attorney to answer and take care of in the lump. He is studying the passions themselves, when he should be inquiring into the debates among men which arise from them. He knows the argument of each of the orations of Demosthenes and Tully, but not one case in the reports of our own courts. No one ever took him for a fool, but none, except his intimate friends, know he has a great deal of wit. This turn makes him at once both disinterested and

Game Act. Laws dating from very early times and regulating the licence to kill game.

Humoursome. Capricious.

Aristotle and Longinus. Aristotle's *Poetics* and Longinus on the *Sublime* are classics of literary criticism.

Littleton or Coke. Famous writers on law.

Demosthenes and Tully. Demosthenes and M. Tullius Cicero, the great orators of Athens and Rome respectively.

Wit. Cleverness.

agreeable: as few of his thoughts are drawn from business, they are most of them fit for conversation. His taste of books is a little too just for the age he lives in; he has read all, but approves of very few. His familiarity with the customs, manners, actions, and writings of the ancients, makes him a very delicate observer of what occurs to him in the present world. He is an excellent critic, and the time of the play is his hour of business; exactly at five he passes through New Inn, crosses through Russell Court, and takes a turn at Will's until the play begins; he has his shoes rubbed and his periwig powdered at the barber's as you go into the Rose. It is for the good of the audience when he is at a play, for the actors have an ambition to please him.

The person of next consideration is Sir Andrew Freeport, a merchant of great eminence in the city of London. A person of indefatigable industry, strong reason, and great experience. His notions of trade are noble and generous, and (as every rich man has usually some sly way of jesting, which would make no great figure were he not a rich man) he calls the sea the British Common. He is acquainted with commerce in all its parts, and will tell you that it is a stupid and barbarous way to extend dominion by arms; for true power is to be got by arts and industry. He will often argue, that if this part of our trade were well cultivated, we should gain from one nation; and if another, from another. I have heard him prove, that diligence makes more lasting

The Rose. The Rose tavern was frequented by actors.

acquisitions than valour, and that sloth has ruined
more nations than the sword. He abounds in several
frugal maxims, amongst which the greatest favourite
is, " A penny saved is a penny got."   A general
trader of good sense is pleasanter company than a
general scholar; and Sir Andrew having a natural
unaffected eloquence, the perspicuity of his discourse gives the same pleasure that wit would in
another man. He has made his fortunes himself;
and says that England may be richer than other
kingdoms, by as plain methods as he himself is richer
than other men; though, at the same time, I can say
this of him, that there is not a point in the compass
but blows home a ship in which he is an owner.

Next to Sir Andrew in the club-room sits Captain
Sentry, a gentleman of great courage, good understanding, but invincible modesty. He is one of those
that deserve very well, but are very awkward at
putting their talents within the observation of such
as should take notice of them. He was some years
a captain, and behaved himself with great gallantry
in several engagements, and at several sieges; but
having a small estate of his own, and being next
heir to Sir Roger, he has quitted a way of life in
which no man can rise suitably to his merit, who is
not something of a courtier, as well as a soldier. I
have heard him often lament, that in a profession
where merit is placed in so conspicuous a view,
impudence should get the better of modesty. When
he has talked to this purpose, I never heard him
make a sour expression, but frankly confess that he

left the world because he was not fit for it. A strict honesty and an even regular behaviour, are in themselves obstacles to him that must press through crowds, who endeavour at the same end with himself, the favour of a commander. He will however, in his way of talk, excuse generals, for not disposing according to men's desert, or inquiring into it: For, says he, that great man who has a mind to help me, has as many to break through to come at me, as I have to come at him: Therefore he will conclude, that the man who would make a figure, especially in a military way, must get over all false modesty, and assist his patron against the importunity of other pretenders, by a proper assurance in his own vindication. He says it is a civil cowardice to be backward in asserting what you ought to expect, as it is a military fear to be slow in attacking when it is your duty. With this candour does the gentleman speak of himself and others. The same frankness runs through all his conversation. The military part of his life has furnished him with many adventures, in the relation of which he is very agreeable to the company; for he is never overbearing, though accustomed to command men in the utmost degree below him; nor ever too obsequious, from an habit of obeying men highly above him.

But that our society may not appear a set of humorists, unacquainted with the gallantries and

---

The world. I.e., of public life.
Own vindication. Self-assertion.
Civil. Civilian.   *Humorists.* Eccentrics.

pleasures of the age, we have among us the gallant
Will Honeycomb, a gentleman who, according to
his years, should be in the decline of his life, but
having ever been very careful of his person, and
always had a very easy fortune, time has made but
a very little impression, either by wrinkles on his
forehead, or traces in his brain. His person is well
turned, of a good height. He is very ready at that
sort of discourse with which men usually entertain
women. He has all his life dressed very well, and
remembers habits as others do men. He can smile
when one speaks to him, and laughs easily. He knows
the history of every mode, and can inform you from
which of the French ladies our wives and daughters
had this manner of curling their hair, that way of
placing their hoods, and whose vanity to show her
foot made that part of the dress so short in such a
year. In a word, all his conversation and knowledge
have been in the female world: as other men of
his age will take notice to you what such a minister
said upon such and such an occasion, he will tell
you when the Duke of Monmouth danced at court,
such a woman was then smitten, another was taken
with him at the head of his troop in the Park. In all
these important relations, he has ever about the
same time received a kind glance or a blow of a fan
from some celebrated beauty, mother of the present
Lord Such-a-one. This way of talking of his very
much enlivens the conversation among us of a more

Turned. Shaped.
Habits. Clothes; *i.e.*, fashions.

sedate turn; and I find there is not one of the company, but myself, who rarely speak at all, but speaks of him as of that sort of man who is usually called a well-bred Fine Gentleman. To conclude his character, where women are not concerned, he is an honest worthy man.

I cannot tell whether I am to account him whom I am next to speak of, as one of our company; for he visits us but seldom, but, when he does, it adds to every man else a new enjoyment of himself. He is a clergyman, a very philosophic man, of general learning, great sanctity of life, and the most exact good breeding. He has the misfortune to be of a very weak constitution, and consequently cannot accept of such cares and business as preferments in his function would oblige him to: he is therefore among divines what a chamber-counsellor is among lawyers. The probity of his mind, and the integrity of his life, create him followers, as being eloquent or loud advances others. He seldom introduces the subject he speaks upon; but we are so far gone in years, that he observes when he is among us, an earnestness to have him fall on some divine topic, which he always treats with much authority, as one who has no interests in this world, as one who is hastening to the object of all his wishes, and conceives hope from his decays and infirmities. These are my ordinary companions. R.

Chamber-counsellor. Barrister whose practice is confined to consultations.
Divine topic. Topic of divinity.

No. 106.   MONDAY, JULY 2

Hinc tibi copia
Manabit ad plenum, benigno
Ruris honorum opulenta cornu.
HOR. *Od.* xvii. l. i. ver. 14.

Here to thee shall plenty flow,
And all her riches show,
To raise the honour of the quiet plain.
CREECH.

HAVING often received an invitation from my friend
Sir Roger de Coverley to pass away a month with
him in the country, I last week accompanied him
thither, and am settled with him for some time at
his country-house, where I intend to form several
of my ensuing speculations. Sir Roger, who is very
well acquainted with my humour, lets me rise and
go to bed when I please, dine at his own table or
in my chamber as I think fit, sit still and say nothing
without bidding me be merry. When the gentlemen of the country come to see him, he only shows
me at a distance: as I have been walking in his
fields, I have observed them stealing a sight of me
over an hedge, and have heard the Knight desiring
them not to let me see them, for that I hated to be
stared at.

I am the more at ease in Sir Roger's family, because
it consists of sober and staid persons; for, as the
Knight is the best master in the world, he seldom
changes his servants; and as he is beloved by all

Humour. Disposition.

about him, his servants never care for leaving him; by this means his domestics are all in years, and grown old with their master. You would take his *valet de chambre* for his brother, his butler is grey-headed, his groom is one of the gravest men that I have ever seen, and his coachman has the looks of a privy counsellor. You see the goodness of the master even in the old house-dog, and in a grey pad that is kept in the stable with great care and tenderness out of regard to his past services, though he has been useless for several years.

I could not but observe, with a great deal of pleasure, the joy that appeared in the countenance of these ancient domestics upon my friend's arrival at his country seat. Some of them could not refrain from tears at the sight of their old master; every one of them pressed forward to do something for him, and seemed discouraged if they were not employed. At the same time the good old Knight, with a mixture of the father and the master of the family, tempered the inquiries after his own affairs with several kind questions relating to themselves. This humanity and good-nature engages everybody to him, so that when he is pleasant upon any of them, all his family are in good humour, and none so much as the person whom he diverts himself with: on the contrary, if he coughs, or betrays any infirmity of old age, it is easy for a stander-by to observe a secret concern in the looks of all his servants.

Pad. Easy-paced horse.
Is pleasant upon. Jokes with; chaffs.

"Every one of them press'd forward to do something for him"

My worthy friend has put me under the particular care of his butler, who is a very prudent man, and, as well as the rest of his fellow-servants, wonderfully desirous of pleasing me, because they have often heard their master talk of me as of his particular friend.

My chief companion, when Sir Roger is diverting himself in the woods or the fields, is a very venerable man who is ever with Sir Roger, and has lived at his house in the nature of a chaplain above thirty years. This gentleman is a person of good sense and some learning, of a very regular life, and obliging conversation: he heartily loves Sir Roger, and knows that he is very much in the old Knight's esteem, so that he lives in the family rather as a relation than a dependent.

I have observed in several of my papers, that my friend Sir Roger, amidst all his good qualities, is something of an humorist; and that his virtues, as well as imperfections, are, as it were, tinged by a certain extravagance, which makes them particularly *his*, and distinguishes them from those of other men. This cast of mind, as it is generally very innocent in itself, so it renders his conversation highly agreeable, and more delightful than the same degree of sense and virtue would appear in their common and ordinary colours. As I was walking with him last night, he asked me how I liked the good man whom I have just now mentioned? And without staying for my answer, told me, that he was afraid of being insulted with Latin and Greek at his own table; for which reason he desired a particular friend of his at the University to find him out a clergyman rather of plain sense than much learning, of a good aspect, a clear voice, a sociable temper, and, if possible, a man that understood a little of backgammon. My friend, says Sir Roger, found me out this gentleman, who, besides the endowments required of him, is, they tell me, a good scholar, though he does not show it: I have

Conversation. Manner of conducting oneself in intercourse. Compare note on p. 40.

Humorist. Whimsical person.

given him the parsonage of the parish; and because
I know his value, have settled upon him a good
annuity for life. If he outlives me, he shall find that
he was higher in my esteem than perhaps he thinks
he is. He has now been with me thirty years; and
though he does not know I have taken notice of it,
has never in all that time asked anything of me for
himself, though he is every day soliciting me for
something in behalf of one or other of my tenants,
his parishioners. There has not been a law-suit
in the parish since he has lived among them: if any
dispute arises they apply themselves to him for the
decision; if they do not acquiesce in his judgment,
which I think never happened above once or twice
at most, they appeal to me. At his first settling with
me, I made him a present of all the good sermons
which have been printed in English, and only begged of
him that every Sunday he would pronounce one of them
in the pulpit. Accordingly, he has digested them into
such a series, that they follow one another naturally,
and make a continued system of practical divinity.

As Sir Roger was going on in his story, the gentleman we were talking of came up to us; and upon
the Knight's asking him who preached to-morrow
(for it was Saturday night,) told us, the Bishop of
St. Asaph in the morning, and Dr. South in the
afternoon. He then showed us his list of preachers
for the whole year, where I saw with a great deal of
pleasure Archbishop Tillotson, Bishop Saunderson,
Dr. Barrow, Dr. Calamy, with several living authors

Digested. Arranged.

who have published discourses of practical divinity. I no sooner saw this venerable man in the pulpit, but I very much approved of my friend's insisting upon the qualifications of a good aspect and a clear voice; for I was so charmed with the gracefulness of his figure and delivery, as well as with the discourses he pronounced, that I think I never passed any time more to my satisfaction. A sermon repeated after this manner, is like the composition of a poet in the mouth of a graceful actor.

I could heartily wish that more of our country clergy would follow this example; and, instead of wasting their spirits in laborious compositions of their own, would endeavour after a handsome elocution, and all those other talents that are proper to enforce what has been penned by greater masters. This would not only be more easy to themselves, but more edifying to the people.   L.

No. 107.   TUESDAY, JULY 3

> *Aesopo ingentem statuam posuere Attici,*
> *Servumque collocârunt aeterna in basi,*
> *Patere honoris scirent ut cunctis viam.*
>   PHÆDR. *Epilog.* l. 2.

The Athenians erected a large statue to Æsop, and placed him, though a slave, on a lasting pedestal; to show, that the way to honour lies open indifferently to all.

THE reception, manner of attendance, undisturbed freedom and quiet, which I meet with here in the country, has confirmed me in the opinion I always

Handsome elocution. Good style of delivery.

had, that the general corruption of manners in
servants is owing to the conduct of masters. The
aspect of every one in the family carries so much
satisfaction, that it appears he knows the happy
lot which has befallen him in being a member of it.
There is one particular which I have seldom seen
but at Sir Roger's; it is usual in all other places,
that servants fly from the parts of the house through
which their master is passing; on the contrary,
here they industriously place themselves in his way;
and it is on both sides, as it were, understood as
a visit when the servants appear without calling.
This proceeds from the humane and equal temper
of the man of the house, who also perfectly well
knows how to enjoy a great estate, with such economy
as ever to be much beforehand. This makes his own
mind untroubled, and consequently unapt to vent
peevish expressions, or give passionate or inconsistent orders to those about him. Thus respect
and love go together; and a certain cheerfulness in
performance of their duty is the particular distinction
of the lower part of this family. When a servant is
called before his master, he does not come with an
expectation to hear himself rated for some trivial
fault, threatened to be stripped or used with any
other unbecoming language, which mean masters
often give to worthy servants; but it is often to

Family. Family in its original Latin meaning of *household.*
Industriously. On purpose.
With such economy . . . beforehand. With such thrift as
always to be well within his income.
Stripped. Discharged.

know what road he took, that he came so readily back according to order; whether he passed by such a ground; if the old man who rents it is in good health; or whether he gave Sir Roger's love to him, or the like.

A man who preserves a respect, founded on his benevolence to his dependents, lives rather like a prince than a master in his family; his orders are received as favours, rather than duties; and the distinction of approaching him is part of the reward for executing what is commanded by him.

There is another circumstance in which my friend excels in his management, which is the manner of rewarding his servants: he has ever been of opinion, that giving his cast clothes to be worn by valets has a very ill effect upon little minds, and creates a silly sense of equality between the parties, in persons affected only with outward things. I have heard him often pleasant on this occasion, and describe a young gentleman abusing his man in that coat, which a month or two before was the most pleasing distinction he was conscious of in himself. He would turn his discourse still more pleasantly upon the ladies' bounties of this kind; and I have heard him say he knew a fine woman, who distributed rewards and punishments in giving becoming or unbecoming dresses to her maids.

But my good friend is above these little instances of good-will, in bestowing only trifles on his servants; a good servant to him is sure of having it in his

Pleasant on this occasion. Joking on this topic.

choice very soon of being no servant at all. As I before observed, he is so good an husband, and knows so thoroughly that the skill of the purse is the cardinal virtue of this life: I say, he knows so well that frugality is the support of generosity, that he can often spare a large fine when a tenement falls, and give that settlement to a good servant, who has a mind to go into the world, or make a stranger pay the fine to that servant, for his more comfortable maintenance, if he stays in his service.

A man of honour and generosity considers it would be miserable to himself to have no will but that of another, though it were of the best person breathing, and for that reason goes on as fast as he is able to put his servants into independent livelihoods. The greatest part of Sir Roger's estate is tenanted by persons who have served himself or his ancestors. It was to me extremely pleasant to observe the visitants from several parts to welcome his arrival in the country; and all the difference that I could take notice of between the late servants who came to see him, and those who stayed in the family, was, that these latter were looked upon as finer gentlemen and better courtiers.

This manumission and placing them in a way of livelihood, I look upon as only what is due to a good servant, which encouragement will make his successor be as diligent, as humble, and as ready as he was.

So good an husband. So thrifty a man.
Fine. Premium paid by new tenant to landlord.
Manumission. Release from service.

There is something wonderful in the narrowness of those minds, which can be pleased, and be barren of bounty to those who please them.

One might, on this occasion, recount the sense that great persons in all ages have had of the merit of their dependents, and the heroic services which men have done their masters in the extremity of their fortunes; and shown, to their undone patrons, that fortune was all the difference between them; but as I design this my speculation only as a gentle admonition to thankless masters, I shall not go out of the occurrences of common life, but assert it as a general observation, that I never saw but in Sir Roger's family, and one or two more, good servants treated as they ought to be. Sir Roger's kindness extends to their children's children, and this very morning he sent his coachman's grandson to prentice. I shall conclude this paper with an account of a picture in his gallery, where there are many which will deserve my future observation.

At the very upper end of this handsome structure I saw the portraiture of two young men standing in a river, the one naked, the other in a livery. The person supported seemed half dead, but still so much alive as to show in his face exquisite joy and love towards the other. I thought the fainting figure resembled my friend Sir Roger; and looking at the butler, who stood by me, for an account of it, he informed me that the person in the livery was a

Undone. Ruined.
All the difference. The only difference.

servant of Sir Roger's, who stood on the shore while his master was swimming, and observing him taken with some sudden illness, and sink under water, jumped in and saved him. He told me Sir Roger took off the dress he was in as soon as he came home, and by a great bounty at that time, followed by his favour ever since, had made him master of that pretty seat which we saw at a distance as we came to this house. I remembered indeed Sir Roger said there lived a very worthy gentleman, to whom he was highly obliged, without mentioning anything further. Upon my looking a little dissatisfied at some part of the picture, my attendant informed me that it was against Sir Roger's will, and at the earnest request of the gentleman himself, that he was drawn in the habit in which he had saved his master. R.

No. 108. WEDNESDAY, JULY 4

Gratis anhelans, multa agendo nihil agens.
PHÆDR. *Fab.* v. l. 2.

Out of breath to no purpose, and very busy about nothing.

As I was yesterday morning walking with Sir Roger before his house, a country fellow brought him a huge fish, which, he told him, Mr. William Wimble had caught that very morning; and that he presented it, with his service to him, and intended to

Took off the dress. Dress=livery: *i.e.*, would not allow him to remain a servant.
Habit. Dress.

come and dine with him. At the same time he delivered a letter which my friend read to me as soon as the messenger left him.

SIR ROGER,

I desire you to accept of a jack, which is the best I have caught this season. I intend to come and stay with you a week, and see how the perch bite in the Black River. I observed with some concern, the last time I saw you upon the bowling-green, that your whip wanted a lash to it; I will bring half a dozen with me that I twisted last week, which I hope will serve you all the time you are in the country. I have not been out of the saddle for six days last past, having been at Eton with Sir John's eldest son. He takes to his learning hugely. I am, Sir,

Your humble servant,

WILL WIMBLE.

This extraordinary letter, and message that accompanied it, made me very curious to know the character and quality of the gentleman who sent them; which I found to be as follows. Will Wimble is younger brother to a baronet, and descended of the ancient family of the Wimbles. He is now between forty and fifty; but, being bred to no business and born to no estate, he generally lives with his elder brother as superintendent of his game. He hunts a pack of dogs better than any man in the country, and is very famous for finding out a hare. He is extremely well-versed in all the little handicrafts of an idle man: he makes a May-fly to a miracle; and furnishes the whole country with

Jack. Pike.   *Country.* Country-side.

angle-rods. As he is a good-natured officious fellow, and very much esteemed upon account of his family, he is a welcome guest at every house, and keeps up a good correspondence among all the gentlemen about him. He carries a tulip-root in his pocket from one to another, or exchanges a puppy between a couple of friends that live perhaps in the opposite sides of the county. Will is a particular favourite of all the young heirs, whom he frequently obliges with a net that he has weaved, or a setting dog that he has made himself: he now and then presents a pair of garters of his own knitting to their mothers or sisters; and raises a great deal of mirth among them, by inquiring as often as he meets them *how they wear*? These gentleman-like manufactures and obliging little humours make Will the darling of the country.

Sir Roger was proceeding in the character of him, when we saw him make up to us with two or three hazel-twigs in his hand, that he had cut in Sir Roger's woods, as he came through them in his way to the house. I was very much pleased to observe on one side the hearty and sincere welcome with which Sir Roger received him, and on the other, the secret joy which his guest discovered at sight of the good old Knight. After the first salutes were over, Will desired Sir Roger to lend him one of his servants to carry a set of shuttlecocks he had with him in

Officious. Obliging.
Correspondence. Inter-communication.
Made. Trained.   *Discovered.* Showed.

a little box to a lady that lived about a mile off, to whom it seems he had promised such a present for above this half-year. Sir Roger's back was no sooner turned, but honest Will began to tell me of a large cock pheasant that he had sprung in one of the neighbouring woods, with two or three other adventures of the same nature. Odd and uncommon characters are the game that I look for, and most delight in; for which reason I was as much pleased with the novelty of the person that talked to me, as he could be for his life with the springing of a pheasant, and therefore listened to him with more than ordinary attention.

In the midst of his discourse the bell rung to dinner, where the gentleman I have been speaking of had the pleasure of seeing the huge jack, he had caught, served up for the first dish in a most sumptuous manner. Upon our sitting down to it he gave us a long account how he had hooked it, played with it, foiled it, and at length drew it out upon the bank, with several other particulars that lasted all the first course. A dish of wild-fowl that came afterwards furnished conversation for the rest of the dinner, which concluded with a late invention of Will's for improving the quail-pipe.

Upon withdrawing into my room after dinner, I was secretly touched with compassion towards the honest gentleman that had dined with us; and could not but consider with a great deal of concern,

Foiled. Rendered helpless.
Quail-pipe. Device for decoying quails.

how so good an heart and such busy hands were
wholly employed in trifles; that so much humanity
should be so little beneficial to others, and so much
industry so little advantageous to himself. The
same temper of mind and application to affairs,
might have recommended him to the public esteem,
and have raised his fortune in another station of
life. What good to his country or himself might not
a trader or merchant have done with such useful
though ordinary qualifications?

Will Wimble's is the case of many a younger
brother of a great family, who had rather see their
children starve like gentlemen, than thrive in a
trade or profession that is beneath their quality.
This humour fills several parts of Europe with pride
and beggary. It is the happiness of a trading nation,
like ours, that the younger sons, though incapable
of any liberal art or profession, may be placed in
such a way of life, as may perhaps enable them to
vie with the best of their family : accordingly we find
several citizens that were launched into the world
with narrow fortunes, rising by an honest industry
to greater estates than those of their elder brothers.
It is not improbable but Will was formerly tried
at divinity, law, or physic; and that, finding his
genius did not lie that way, his parents gave him up
at length to his own inventions; but certainly,
however improper he might have been for studies
of a higher nature, he was perfectly well turned for
the occupations of trade and commerce. As I think

Humour. Prejudice.　　*Turned.* Fitted by nature.

this is a point which cannot be too much inculcated, I shall desire my reader to compare what I have here written with what I have said in my twenty-first speculation.

L.

No. 109. THURSDAY, JULY 5

Abnormis sapiens.
HOR. *Sat.* ii. l. 2. ver. 3.
Of plain good sense, untutor'd in the schools.

I WAS this morning walking in the gallery when Sir Roger entered at the end opposite to me, and advancing towards me, said he was glad to meet me among his relations the De Coverleys, and hoped I liked the conversation of so much good company, who were as silent as myself. I knew he alluded to the pictures, and as he is a gentleman who does not a little value himself upon his ancient descent, I expected he would give me some account of them. We were now arrived at the upper end of the gallery, when the Knight faced towards one of the pictures, and, as we stood before it, he entered into the matter, after his blunt way of saying things, as they occur to his imagination, without regular introduction, or care to preserve the appearance of chain of thought.

"It is," said he, "worth while to consider the force of dress; and how the persons of one age differ from those of another, merely by that only. One may observe also, that the general fashion of one age has been followed by one particular set of people

Conversation. Intercourse with. Compare note on p. 28.

in another, and by them preserved from one generation to another. Thus the vast jetting coat and small bonnet, which was the habit in Harry the Seventh's time, is kept on in the yeomen of the guard; not without a good and politic view, because they look a foot taller, and a foot and an half broader: besides that the cap leaves the face expanded, and consequently more terrible, and fitter to stand at the entrances of palaces.

" This predecessor of ours, you see, is dressed after this manner, and his cheeks would be no larger than mine, were he in a hat as I am. He was the last man that won a prize in the tilt-yard (which is now a common street before Whitehall). You see the broken lance that lies there by his right foot; he shivered that lance of his adversary all to pieces; and bearing himself, look you, sir, in this manner, at the same time he came within the target of the gentleman who rode against him, and taking him with incredible force before him on the pommel of his saddle, he in that manner rid the tournament over, with an air that showed he did it rather to perform the rule of the lists, than expose his enemy; however, it appeared he knew how to make use of a victory, and with a gentle trot he marched up to a gallery where their mistress sat (for they were rivals) and let him down with laudable courtesy and pardonable insolence. I don't know but it might be exactly where the coffee-house is now.

Jetting. Bulging.	*Target.* Targe or small shield.
Tournament. Lists.	*Insolence.* Triumph.

" You are to know this my ancestor was not only of a military genius, but fit also for the arts of peace, for he played on the bass-viol as well as any gentleman at court; you see where his viol hangs by his basket-hilt sword. The action at the tilt-yard you may be sure won the fair lady, who was a maid of honour, and the greatest beauty of her time; here she stands the next picture. You see, sir, my great-great-great-grandmother has on the new-fashioned petticoat, except that the modern is gathered at the waist: my grandmother appears as if she stood in a large drum, whereas the ladies now walk as if they were in a go-cart. For all this lady was bred at court, she became an excellent country wife, she brought ten children, and when I show you the library, you shall see in her own hand (allowing for the difference of the language) the best receipt now in England both for an hasty-pudding and a white-pot.

" If you please to fall back a little, because it is necessary to look at the three next pictures at one view: these are three sisters. She on the right hand, who is so beautiful, died a maid; the next to her, still handsomer, had the same fate, against her will; this homely thing in the middle had both their portions added to her own, and was stolen by a neighbouring gentleman, a man of stratagem and resolution, for he poisoned three mastiffs to come at her, and knocked down two deer-stealers in carrying

Bass-viol. Violoncello.
For all. In spite of the fact that.

her off. Misfortunes happen in all families: the theft of this romp and so much money, was no great matter to our estate. But the next heir that possessed it was this soft gentleman, whom you see there: observe the small buttons, the little boots, the laces, the slashes about his clothes, and above all the posture he is drawn in, (which to be sure was his own choosing;) you see he sits with one hand on a desk writing and looking as it were another way, like an easy writer, or a sonneteer: he was one of those that had too much wit to know how to live in the world; he was a man of no justice, but great good manners; he ruined everybody that had anything to do with him, but never said a rude thing in his life; the most indolent person in the world, he would sign a deed that passed away half his estate with his gloves on, but would not put on his hat before a lady if it were to save his country. He is said to be the first that made love by squeezing the hand. He left the estate with ten thousand pounds debt upon it, but however by all hands I have been informed that he was every way the finest gentleman in the world. That debt lay heavy on our house for one generation, but it was retrieved by a gift from that honest man you see there, a citizen of our name, but nothing at all akin to us. I know Sir Andrew Freeport has said behind my back, that this man was descended from one of the ten children of the maid of honour I showed you above; but it was never made out. We winked at

Slashes. Ornamental slits in a doublet, etc.

the thing indeed, because money was wanting at that time."

Here I saw my friend a little embarrassed, and turned my face to the next portraiture.

Sir Roger went on with his account of the gallery in the following manner. " This man " (pointing to him I looked at) " I take to be the honour of our house, Sir Humphrey de Coverley; he was in his dealings as punctual as a tradesman, and as generous as a gentleman. He would have thought himself as much undone by breaking his word, as if it were to be followed by bankruptcy. He served his country as knight of this shire to his dying day. He found it no easy matter to maintain an integrity in his words and actions, even in things that regarded the offices which were incumbent upon him, in the care of his own affairs and relations of life, and therefore dreaded (though he had great talents) to go into employments of state, where he must be exposed to the snares of ambition. Innocence of life and great ability were the distinguishing parts of his character; the latter, he had often observed, had led to the destruction of the former, and used frequently to lament that great and good had not the same signification. He was an excellent husbandman, but had resolved not to exceed such a degree of wealth; all above it he bestowed in secret bounties many years after the sum he aimed at for his own use was attained. Yet he did not slacken his industry,

Knight of this shire. M.P. for the county.
Such a degree. A fixed amount.

but to a decent old age spent the life and fortune which was superfluous to himself, in the service of his friends and neighbours."

Here we were called to dinner, and Sir Roger ended the discourse of this gentleman, by telling me, as we followed the servant, that this his ancestor was a brave man, and narrowly escaped being killed in the civil wars; " For," said he, " he was sent out of the field upon a private message, the day before the battle of Worcester." The whim of narrowly escaping by having been within a day of danger, with other matters above mentioned, mixed with good sense, left me at a loss whether I was more delighted with my friend's wisdom or simplicity.

R.

No. 110. FRIDAY, JULY 6

Horror ubique animos, simul ipsa silentia terrent.
VIRG. *Æn*. ii. ver. 755.

All things are full of horror and affright,
And dreadful ev'n the silence of the night.
DRYDEN.

AT a little distance from Sir Roger's house, among the ruins of an old abbey, there is a long walk of aged elms; which are shot up so very high, that when one passes under them, the rooks and crows that rest upon the tops of them seem to be cawing in another region. I am very much delighted with this sort of noise, which I consider as a kind of

Discourse of. Discourse about.
Whim. Absurd notion.

natural prayer to that Being who supplies the wants
of his whole creation, and who, in the beautiful
language of the Psalms, feedeth the young ravens
that call upon him. I like this retirement the better,
because of an ill report it lies under of being *haunted*;
for which reason (as I have been told in the family)
no living creature ever walks in it besides the chaplain. My good friend the butler desired me with a
very grave face not to venture myself in it after
sunset, for that one of the footmen had been almost
frighted out of his wits by a spirit that appeared to
him in the shape of a black horse without an head;
to which he added, that about a month ago one of
the maids coming home late that way with a pail
of milk upon her head, heard such a rustling among
the bushes that she let it fall.

I was taking a walk in this place last night between
the hours of nine and ten, and could not but fancy it
one of the most proper scenes in the world for a
ghost to appear in. The ruins of the abbey are scat-
tered up and down on every side, and half covered
with ivy and elder bushes, the harbours of several
solitary birds which seldom make their appearance
till the dusk of the evening. The place was formerly
a churchyard, and has still several marks in it of
graves and burying-places. There is such an echo
among the old ruins and vaults, that if you stamp
but a little louder than ordinary, you hear the sound
repeated. At the same time the walk of elms, with
the croaking of the ravens which from time to time
are heard from the tops of them, looks exceeding

solemn and venerable. These objects naturally raise seriousness and attention; and when night heightens the awfulness of the place, and pours out her supernumerary horrors upon everything in it, I do not at all wonder that weak minds fill it with spectres and apparitions.

Mr. Locke, in his chapter of the Association of Ideas, has very curious remarks to show how, by the prejudice of education, one idea often introduces into the mind a whole set that bear no resemblance to one another in the nature of things. Among several examples of this kind, he produces the following instance. " The ideas of goblins and sprites have really no more to do with darkness than light: yet let but a foolish maid inculcate these often on the mind of a child, and raise them there together, possibly he shall never be able to separate them again so long as he lives; but darkness shall ever afterwards bring with it those frightful ideas, and they shall be so joined, that he can no more bear the one than the other."

As I was walking in this solitude, where the dusk of the evening conspired with so many other occasions of terror, I observed a cow grazing not far from me, which an imagination that was apt to startle might easily have construed into a black horse without an head: and I dare say the poor footman lost his wits upon some such trivial occasion.

Supernumerary. Additional.
Curious. Interesting.
Prejudice of education. Bent given to the mind by education.

My friend Sir Roger has often told me with a good deal of mirth, that at his first coming to his estate he found three parts of his house altogether useless; that the best room in it had the reputation of being haunted, and by that means was locked up; that noises had been heard in his long gallery, so that he could not get a servant to enter it after eight o'clock at night; that the door of one of the chambers was nailed up, because there went a story in the family that a butler had formerly hanged himself in it; and that his mother, who lived to a great age, had shut up half the rooms in the house, in which either her husband, a son, or daughter had died. The Knight seeing his habitation reduced to so small a compass, and himself in a manner shut out of his own house, upon the death of his mother ordered all the apartments to be flung open, and exorcised by his chaplain, who lay in every room one after another, and by that means dissipated the fears which had so long reigned in the family.

I should not have been thus particular upon these ridiculous horrors, did not I find them so very much prevail in all parts of the country. At the same time I think a person who is thus terrified with the imagination of ghosts and spectres, much more reasonable than one who, contrary to the reports of all historians sacred and profane, ancient and modern, and to the traditions of all nations, thinks the appearance of spirits fabulous and groundless: could not

By that means. Because of that.
Exorcised. Delivered from supernatural influence.

I give myself up to this general testimony of mankind, I should to the relations of particular persons who are now living, and whom I cannot distrust in other matters of fact. I might here add, that not only the historians, to whom we may join the poets, but likewise the philosophers of antiquity have favoured this opinion. Lucretius himself, though by the course of his philosophy he was obliged to maintain that the soul did not exist separate from the body, makes no doubt of the reality of apparitions, and that men have often appeared after their death. This I think very remarkable. He was so pressed with the matter of fact which he could not have the confidence to deny, that he was forced to account for it by one of the most absurd unphilosophical notions that was ever started. He tells us, that the surfaces of all bodies are perpetually flying off from their respective bodies, one after another; and that these surfaces or thin cases, that included each other whilst they were joined in the body like the coats of an onion, are sometimes seen entire when they are separated from it; by which means we often behold the shapes and shadows of persons who are either dead or absent.

I shall dismiss this paper with a story out of Josephus, not so much for the sake of the story itself as for the moral reflections with which the author concludes it, and which I shall here set down in his own words. " Glaphyra the daughter of King

Lucretius. Roman philosopher-poet: 95–52 B.C.
Pressed. Compelled.

Archelaus, after the death of her two first husbands
(being married to a third, who was brother to her
first husband, and so passionately in love with her
that he turned off his former wife to make room for
this marriage) had a very odd kind of dream. She
fancied that she saw her first husband coming towards
her, and that she embraced him with great tenderness; when in the midst of the pleasure which she
expressed at the sight of him, he reproached her
after the following manner: 'Glaphyra,' says he,
'thou hast made good the old saying, That women
are not to be trusted. Was not I the husband of
thy virginity? Have I not children by thee? How
couldst thou forget our loves so far as to enter into
a second marriage, and after that into a third, nay
to take for thy husband a man who has so shame-
fully crept into the bed of his brother? However,
for the sake of our passed loves, I shall free thee
from thy present reproach, and make thee mine
for ever.' Glaphyra told this dream to several women
of her acquaintance, and died soon after. I thought
this story might not be impertinent in this place,
wherein I speak of those kings: besides that the
example deserves to be taken notice of, as it contains
a most certain proof of the immortality of the soul,
and of Divine Providence. If any man thinks these
facts incredible, let him enjoy his own opinion to
himself, but let him not endeavour to disturb the
belief of others, who by instances of this nature are
excited to the study of virtue."   L.

No. 112.   MONDAY, JULY 9

> Ἀθανάτους μὲν πρῶτα θεούς, νόμῳ ὡς διάκειται,
> Τίμα.
>
> PYTHAG.
>
> First, in obedience to thy country's rites,
> Worship the immortal Gods.

I AM always very well pleased with a country Sunday;
and think, if keeping holy the seventh day were
only a human institution, it would be the best method
that could have been thought of for the polishing
and civilising of mankind. It is certain the country
people would soon degenerate into a kind of savages
and barbarians, were there not such frequent returns
of a stated time, in which the whole village meet
together with their best faces, and in their cleanliest
habits, to converse with one another upon indifferent
subjects, hear their duties explained to them, and
join together in adoration of the Supreme Being.
Sunday clears away the rust of the whole week, not
only as it refreshes in their minds the notions of
religion, but as it puts both the sexes upon appearing
in their most agreeable forms, and exerting all such
qualities as are apt to give them a figure in the eye
of the village. A country fellow distinguishes himself
as much in the churchyard, as a citizen does upon
the 'Change, the whole parish politics being generally
discussed in that place, either after sermon or before
the bell rings.

My friend Sir Roger, being a good churchman, has

Only. Merely.
Puts both the sexes upon appearing. Impels them to appear.

beautified the inside of his church with several texts of his own choosing: he has likewise given a handsome pulpit cloth, and railed in the communion-table at his own expense. He has often told me, that at his coming to his estate he found his parishioners very irregular; and that, in order to make them kneel and join in the responses, he gave every one of them a hassock and a common-prayer-book; and at the same time employed an itinerant singing-master, who goes about the country for that purpose, to instruct them rightly in the tunes of the psalms; upon which they now very much value themselves, and indeed outdo most of the country churches that I have ever heard.

As Sir Roger is landlord to the whole congregation, he keeps them in very good order, and will suffer nobody to sleep in it besides himself; for, if by chance he has been surprised into a short nap at sermon, upon recovering out of it he stands up and looks about him, and if he sees anybody else nodding, either wakes them himself, or sends his servants to them. Several other of the old Knight's particularities break out upon these occasions: sometimes he will be lengthening out a verse in the singing psalms, half a minute after the rest of the congregation have done with it; sometimes, when he is pleased with the matter of his devotion, he pronounces " Amen " three or four times to the same prayer; and sometimes stands up when everybody else is upon their knees, to count the congregation, or see if any of his tenants are missing.

Particularities. Peculiarities.

I was yesterday very much surprised to hear my old friend, in the midst of the service, calling out to one John Matthews to mind what he was about, and not disturb the congregation. This John Matthews it seems is remarkable for being an idle fellow, and at that time was kicking his heels for his diversion. This authority of the Knight, though exerted in that odd manner which accompanies him in all circumstances of life, has a very good effect upon the parish, who are not polite enough to see anything ridiculous in his behaviour; besides that, the general good sense and worthiness of his character makes his friends observe these little singularities as foils, that rather set off than blemish his good qualities.

As soon as the sermon is finished, nobody presumes to stir till Sir Roger is gone out of the church. The Knight walks down from his seat in the chancel between a double row of his tenants, that stand bowing to him on each side; and every now and then inquires how such an one's wife, or mother, or son, or father do, whom he does not see at church; which is understood as a secret reprimand to the person that is absent.

The chaplain has often told me, that upon a catechising day, when Sir Roger has been pleased with a boy that answers well, he has ordered a bible to be given him next day for his encouragement; and sometimes accompanies it with a flitch of bacon to his mother. Sir Roger has likewise added five pounds a year to the clerk's place: and that he may encourage the young fellows to make themselves perfect in the church service, has promised upon the death of the present incumbent, who is very old, to bestow it according to merit.

The fair understanding between Sir Roger and his chaplain, and their mutual concurrence in doing good, is the more remarkable, because the very next village is famous for the differences and contentions that arise between the parson and the squire, who live in a perpetual state of war. The parson is always preaching at the squire, and the squire to be revenged on the parson never comes to church. The squire has made all his tenants atheists and tithe-stealers; while the parson instructs them every Sunday in the dignity of his order, and insinuates to them in almost every sermon, that he is a better man than his patron. In short, matters are come to such an extremity, that the squire has not said his prayers either in public or private this halfyear; and that the parson threatens him, if he does not mend his manners, to pray for him in the face of the whole congregation.

Feuds of this nature, though too frequent in the country, are very fatal to the ordinary people; who are so used to be dazzled with riches, that they pay as much deference to the understanding of a man of an estate, as of a man of learning; and are very hardly brought to regard any truth, how important soever it may be, that is preached to them, when they know there are several men of five hundred a year, who do not believe it.　　　　L.

Incumbent. Holder of the post.

No. 113.   TUESDAY, JULY 10

Haerent infixi pectore vultus.
                                    VIRG. *Æn.* iv. ver. 4.
Her looks were deep imprinted in his heart.

IN my first description of the company in which I
pass most of my time, it may be remembered that
I mentioned a great affliction which my friend Sir
Roger had met with in his youth; which was no
less than a disappointment in love. It happened
this evening that we fell into a very pleasing walk
at a distance from his house: as soon as we came
into it, " It is," quoth the good old man, looking
round him with a smile, " very hard, that any part
of my land should be settled upon one who has used
me so ill as the perverse widow did; and yet I am
sure I could not see a sprig of any bough of this
whole walk of trees, but I should reflect upon her
and her severity. She has certainly the finest hand
of any woman in the world. You are to know this
was the place wherein I used to muse upon her;
and by that custom I can never come into it, but
the same tender sentiments revive in my mind,
as if I had actually walked with that beautiful
creature under these shades. I have been fool enough
to carve her name on the bark of several of these
trees; so unhappy is the condition of men in love,
to attempt the removing of their passions by the
methods which serve only to imprint it deeper.

Settled. An obscure expression. Possibly it means " bound
up with."

She has certainly the finest hand of any woman in the world."

Here followed a profound silence; and I was not displeased to observe my friend falling so naturally into a discourse, which I had ever before taken notice he industriously avoided. After a very long pause he entered upon an account of this great circumstance in his life, with an air which I thought raised my idea of him above what I had ever had before; and gave me the picture of that cheerful mind of his, before it received that stroke which has ever since affected his words and actions. But he went on as follows.

"I came to my estate in my twenty-second year, and resolved to follow the steps of the most worthy of my ancestors who have inhabited this spot of earth before me, in all the methods of hospitality and good neighbourhood, for the sake of my fame; and in country sports and recreations, for the sake of my health. In my twenty-third year I was obliged to serve as sheriff of the county; and, in my servants, officers, and whole equipage, indulged the pleasure of a young man (who did not think ill of his own person) in taking that public occasion of showing my figure and behaviour to advantage. You may easily imagine to yourself what appearance I made, who am pretty tall, rid well, and was very well dressed, at the head of a whole county, with music before me, a feather in my hat, and my horse well bitted. I can assure you I was not a little pleased

Rid. Rode.

with the kind looks and glances I had from all the
balconies and windows as I rode to the hall where
the assizes were held.   But when I came there, a
beautiful creature in a widow's habit sat in court,
to hear the event of a cause concerning her dower.
This commanding creature (who was born for the
destruction of all who behold her) put on such a
resignation in her countenance, and bore the whispers
of all around the court, with such a pretty uneasiness,
I warrant you, and then recovered herself from one
eye to another, till she was perfectly confused by
meeting something so wistful in all she encountered,
that at last, with a murrain to her, she cast her
bewitching eye upon me.   I no sooner met it, but I
bowed like a great surprised booby;   and knowing
her cause to be the first which came on, I cried,
like a captivated calf as I was, ' Make way for the
defendant's witnesses.'   This sudden partiality made
all the county immediately see the sheriff was also
become a slave to the fine widow.   During the time
her cause was upon trial, she behaved herself, I
warrant you, with such a deep attention to her
business, took opportunities to have little billets
handed to her counsel, then would be in such a
pretty confusion, occasioned, you must know, by
acting before so much company, that not only I,
but the whole court was prejudiced in her favour;
and all that the next heir to her husband had to
urge, was thought so groundless and frivolous, that
when it came to her counsel to reply, there was not

Dower. Widow's portion of her husband's property.

half so much said as every one besides in the court thought he could have urged to her advantage. You must understand, sir, this perverse woman is one of those unaccountable creatures, that secretly rejoice in the admiration of men, but indulge themselves in no further consequences. Hence it is that she has ever had a train of admirers, and she removes from her slaves in town to those in the country, according to the seasons of the year. She is a reading lady, and far gone in the pleasures of friendship: she is always accompanied by a confidant, who is witness to her daily protestations against our sex, and consequently a bar to her first steps towards love, upon the strength of her own maxims and declarations.

"However, I must needs say this accomplished mistress of mine has distinguished me above the rest, and has been known to declare Sir Roger de Coverley was the tamest and most humane of all the brutes in the country. I was told she said so, by one who thought he rallied me; but upon the strength of this slender encouragement of being thought least detestable, I made new liveries, new-paired my coach-horses, sent them all to town to be bitted, and taught to throw their legs well, and move all together, before I pretended to cross the country, and wait upon her. As soon as I thought my retinue suitable to the character of my fortune and youth, I set out from hence to make my addresses.

Humane. Civilised.   *Rallied.* Bantered.
            Pretended. Presumed.

She began a Discourse to me concerning Love and Honour

The particular skill of this lady has ever been to inflame your wishes, and yet command respect. To make her mistress of this art, she has a greater share of knowledge, wit, and good sense, than is usual even among men of merit. Then she is beautiful beyond the race of women. If you will not let her go on with a certain artifice with her eyes, and the skill of beauty, she will arm herself with her real charms, and strike you with admiration instead of desire. It is certain that if you were to behold the whole woman, there is that dignity in her aspect, that composure in her motion, that complacency in her manner, that if her form makes you hope, her merit makes you fear. But then again she is such a desperate scholar, that no country gentleman can approach her without being a jest. As I was going to tell you, when I came to her house I was admitted to her presence with great civility; at the same time she placed herself to be first seen by me in such an attitude, as I think you call the posture of a picture, that she discovered new charms, and I at last came towards her with such an awe as made me speechless. This she no sooner observed but she made her advantage of it, and began a discourse to me concerning love and honour, as they both are followed by pretenders, and the real votaries to them. When she discussed these points in a discourse, which I verily believe was as learned as the best philosopher in Europe could possibly make, she asked me whether she was so happy as to fall in with my sentiments on these important particulars. Her confidant sat by her, and upon my being in the last confusion and silence, this malicious *aide* of hers turning to her says, ' I am very glad to observe Sir Roger pauses upon this subject, and seems resolved to deliver all his sentiments upon the matter when he pleases to speak.' They both kept their countenances, and after I had sat half an hour meditating how to behave before such profound casuists, I rose up and took my leave. Chance has since that time thrown me very often in her way, and she as often has directed a discourse to

Discovered. Displayed.   *Last*. Utmost.

me which I do not understand. This barbarity has kept me ever at a distance from the most beautiful object my eyes ever beheld. It is thus also she deals with all mankind, and you must make love to her, as you would conquer the sphinx, by posing her. But were she like other women, and that there were any talking to her, how constant must the pleasure of that man be, who would converse with a creature—But, after all, you may be sure her heart is fixed on some one or other; and yet I have been credibly informed—but who can believe half that is said? After she had done speaking to me, she put her hand to her bosom and adjusted her tucker. Then she cast her eyes a little down, upon my beholding her too earnestly. They say she sings excellently: her voice in her ordinary speech has something in it inexpressibly sweet. You must know I dined with her at a public table the day after I first saw her, and she helped me to some tansy in the eye of all the gentlemen in the country. She has certainly the finest hand of any woman in the world. I can assure you, sir, were you to behold her, you would be in the same condition; for as her speech is music, her form is angelic. But I find I grow irregular while I am talking of her; but indeed it would be stupidity to be unconcerned at such perfection. Oh the excellent creature! she is as

Conquer the sphinx, by posing her. Reference to the story of Œdipus, who answered the riddle of the Sphinx, whereupon she destroyed herself " Pose " her, *i.e.*, with a problem she cannot solve.

Irregular. Incoherent.

inimitable to all women, as she is inaccessible to all men."

I found my friend begin to rave, and insensibly led him towards the house, that we might be joined by some other company; and am convinced that the widow is the secret cause of all that inconsistency which appears in some parts of my friend's discourse, though he has so much command of himself as not directly to mention her, yet according to that of Martial, which one knows not how to render into English, *Dum tacet hanc loquitur.* I shall end this paper with that whole epigram, which represents with much humour my honest friend's condition.

> *Quicquid agit Rufus, nihil est, nisi Naevia Rufo,*
> *Si gaudet, si flet, si tacet, hanc loquitur :*
> *Coenat, propinat, poscit, negat, annuit, una est*
> *Naevia; si non sit Naevia, mutus erit.*
> *Scriberet hesternâ patri cùm luce salutem,*
> *Naevia lux, inquit, Naevia numen, ave.*
> *Epig.* lxix. l. 1.

Let Rufus weep, rejoice, stand, sit, or walk,
Still he can nothing but of Nævia talk;
Let him eat, drink, ask questions, or dispute,
Still he must speak of Nævia, or be mute.
He writ to his father, ending with this line,
I am, my lovely Nævia, ever thine.

R.

Insensibly. Without his noticing it.
Martial. Latin satirist: 41-104 A.D.

No. 115.   Thursday, July 12

Ut sit mens sana in corpore sano.
Juv. *Sat.* x. ver. 356.
A healthy body and a mind at ease.

Bodily labour is of two kinds, either that which
a man submits to for his livelihood, or that which
he undergoes for his pleasure. The latter of them
generally changes the name of labour for that of
exercise, but differs only from ordinary labour as
it rises from another motive.

A country life abounds in both these kinds of
labour, and for that reason gives a man a greater
stock of health, and consequently a more perfect
enjoyment of himself, than any other way of life.
I consider the body as a system of tubes and glands,
or to use a more rustic phrase, a bundle of pipes
and strainers, fitted to one another after so wonderful
a manner as to make a proper engine for the soul
to work with. This description does not only com-
prehend the bowels, bones, tendons, veins, nerves,
and arteries, but every muscle and every ligature,
which is a composition of fibres, that are so many
imperceptible tubes or pipes interwoven on all sides
with invisible glands or strainers.

This general idea of a human body, without considering it in its niceties of anatomy, lets us see how
absolutely necessary labour is for the right preservation of it. There must be frequent motions and
agitations, to mix, digest, and separate the juices
contained in it, as well as to clear and cleanse that

infinitude of pipes and strainers of which it is composed, and to give their solid parts a more firm and lasting tone. Labour or exercise ferments the humours, casts them into their proper channels, throws off redundancies, and helps nature in those secret distributions, without which the body cannot subsist in its vigour, nor the soul act with cheerfulness.

I might here mention the effects which this has upon all the faculties of the mind, by keeping the understanding clear, the imagination untroubled, and refining those spirits that are necessary for the proper exertion of our intellectual faculties, during the present laws of union between soul and body. It is to a neglect in this particular, that we must ascribe the spleen, which is so frequent in men of studious and sedentary tempers, as well as the vapours to which those of the other sex are so often subject.

Had not exercise been absolutely necessary for our well-being, nature would not have made the body so proper for it, by giving such an activity to the limbs, and such a pliancy to every part as necessarily produce these compressions, extensions, contortions, dilatations, and all other kinds of motions that are necessary for the preservation of such a system of tubes and glands as has been before mentioned. And that we might not want inducements to engage us in such an exercise of the body as is proper for

Particular. Respect.
Spleen, vapours. Attacks of depression or melancholy.

its welfare, it is so ordered that nothing valuable can be procured without it. Not to mention riches and honour, even food and raiment are not to be come at without the toil of the hands and sweat of the brows. Providence furnishes materials, but expects that we should work them up ourselves. The earth must be laboured before it gives its increase, and when it is forced into its several products, how many hands must they pass through before they are fit for use? Manufactures, trade, and agriculture, naturally employ more than nineteen parts of the species in twenty; and as for those who are not obliged to labour, by the condition in which they are born, they are more miserable than the rest of mankind, unless they indulge themselves in that voluntary labour which goes by the name of exercise.

My friend Sir Roger has been an indefatigable man in business of this kind, and has hung several parts of his house with the trophies of his former labours. The walls of his great hall are covered with the horns of several kinds of deer that he has killed in the chase, which he thinks the most valuable furniture of his house, as they afford him frequent topics of discourse, and show that he has not been idle. At the lower end of the hall is a large otter's skin stuffed with hay, which his mother ordered to be hung up in that manner, and the Knight looks upon it with great satisfaction, because it seems he was but nine years old when his dog killed him. A little room adjoining to the hall is a kind of arsenal

Condition. Rank.

C

filled with guns of several sizes and inventions, with which the Knight has made great havoc in the woods, and destroyed many thousands of pheasants, part-ridges and woodcocks. His stable doors are patched with noses that belonged to foxes of the Knight's own hunting down. Sir Roger showed me one of them, that for distinction sake has a brass nail struck through it, which cost him about fifteen hours' riding, carried him through half a dozen counties, killed him a brace of geldings, and lost above half his dogs. This the Knight looks upon as one of the greatest exploits of his life. The perverse widow, whom I have given some account of, was the death of several foxes; for Sir Roger has told me that in the course of his amours he patched the western door of his stable. Whenever the widow was cruel, the foxes were sure to pay for it. In proportion as his passion for the widow abated and old age came on, he left off fox-hunting; but a hare is not yet safe that sits within ten miles of his house.

There is no kind of exercise which I would so recommend to my readers of both sexes as this of riding, as there is none which so much conduces to health, and is every way accommodated to the body, according to the *idea* which I have given of it. Doctor Sydenham is very lavish in its praises; and if the English reader will see the mechanical effects of it described at length, he may find them in a book published not many years since, under the title of *Medicina Gymnastica*. For my own part,

Patched. Decorated.   *Amours*. Courtship.

when I am in town, for want of these opportunities, I exercise myself an hour every morning upon a dumb bell that is placed in a corner of my room, and pleases me the more because it does everything I require of it in the most profound silence. My landlady and her daughters are so well acquainted with my hours of exercise, that they never come into my room to disturb me whilst I am ringing.

When I was some years younger than I am at present, I used to employ myself in a more laborious diversion, which I learned from a Latin treatise of exercises that is written with great erudition: it is there called the σκιομαχία, or the fighting with a man's own shadow, and consists in the brandishing of two short sticks grasped in each hand, and loaden with plugs of lead at either end. This opens the chest, exercises the limbs, and gives a man all the pleasure of boxing, without the blows. I could wish that several learned men would lay out that time which they employ in controversies and disputes about nothing, in this method of fighting with their own shadows. It might conduce very much to evaporate the spleen, which makes them uneasy to the public as well as to themselves.

To conclude, as I am a compound of soul and body, I consider myself as obliged to a double scheme of duties; and think I have not fulfilled the business of the day when I do not thus employ the one in labour and exercise, as well as the other in study and contemplation.   L.

Uneasy. Trying.

No. 116.   FRIDAY, JULY 13

> *Vocat ingenti clamore Cithaeron,*
> *Taygetique canes.*

VIRG. *Georg.* iii. ver. 43.

The echoing hills and chiding hounds invite.

THOSE who have searched into human nature observe
that nothing so much shows the nobleness of the
soul as that its felicity consists in action. Every man
has such an active principle in him, that he will
find out something to employ himself upon, in what-
ever place or state of life he is posted. I have heard
of a gentleman who was under close confinement
in the Bastile seven years; during which time he
amused himself in scattering a few small pins about
his chamber, gathering them up again, and placing
them in different figures on the arm of a great chair.
He often told his friends afterwards, that unless he
had found out this piece of exercise, he verily believed he should have lost his senses.

After what has been said, I need not inform my
readers that Sir Roger, with whose character I
hope they are at present pretty well acquainted,
has in his youth gone through the whole course of
those rural diversions which the country abounds
in; and which seem to be extremely well suited to
that laborious industry a man may observe here in
a far greater degree than in towns and cities. I have
before hinted at some of my friend's exploits: he

has in his youthful days taken forty coveys of partridges in a season; and tired many a salmon with a line consisting but of a single hair. The constant thanks and good wishes of the neighbourhood always attended him, on account of his remarkable enmity towards foxes; having destroyed more of those vermin in one year, than it was thought the whole country could have produced. Indeed the Knight does not scruple to own among his most intimate friends, that in order to establish his reputation this way, he has secretly sent for great numbers of them out of other counties, which he used to turn loose about the country by night, that he might the better signalise himself in their destruction the next day. His hunting horses were the finest and best managed in all these parts: his tenants are still full of the praises of a grey stone-horse that unhappily staked himself several years since, and was buried with great solemnity in the orchard.

Sir Roger, being at present too old for fox-hunting, to keep himself in action, has disposed of his beagles and got a pack of stop-hounds. What these want in speed, he endeavours to make amends for by the deepness of their mouths and the variety of their notes, which are suited in such manner to each other, that the whole cry makes up a complete

---

Managed. Trained.   *Stone-horse.* Stallion.
Staked. Impaled.
Stop-hounds. Hounds trained to go slowly and stop at a signal from the huntsman.
Mouths. Cry.   *Cry.* Pack.

concert. He is so nice in this particular, that a gentleman having made him a present of a very fine hound
the other day, the Knight returned it by the servant
with a great many expressions of civility; but
desired him to tell his master, that the dog he had
sent was indeed a most excellent bass, but that at
present he only wanted a counter-tenor. Could I
believe my friend had ever read Shakespeare, I
should certainly conclude he had taken the hint
from Theseus in the *Midsummer Night's Dream.*

> My hounds are bred out of the Spartan kind,
> So flu'd, so sanded; and their heads are hung
> With ears that sweep away the morning dew.
> Crook-knee'd and dew-lap'd like Thessalian bulls,
> Slow in pursuit, but match'd in mouths like bells,
> Each under each: a cry more tuneable
> Was never halloo'd to, nor cheer'd with horn.

Sir Roger is so keen at this sport, that he has been
out almost every day since I came down; and upon
the chaplain's offering to lend me his easy pad, I was
prevailed on yesterday morning to make one of the
company. I was extremely pleased, as we rid along,
to observe the general benevolence of all the neighbourhood towards my friend. The farmer's sons
thought themselves happy if they could open a gate
for the good old Knight as he passed by; which he
generally requited with a nod or a smile, and a kind
inquiry after their fathers and uncles.

After we had rid about a mile from home, we came
upon a large heath, and the sportsmen began to

Nice. Precise, fastidious.   *Counter-tenor.* Alto.
Benevolence. Good-will.

beat. They had done so for some time, when, as I
was at a little distance from the rest of the company,
I saw a hare pop out from a small furze-brake almost
under my horse's feet. I marked the way she took,
which I endeavoured to make the company sensible
of by extending my arm; but to no purpose, until
Sir Roger, who knows that none of my extraordinary
motions are insignificant, rode up to me, and asked
me if puss was gone that way? Upon my answering
" Yes," he immediately called in the dogs, and put
them upon the scent. As they were going off, I heard
one of the country fellows muttering to his companion, "That it was a wonder they had not lost all
their sport, for want of the silent gentleman's crying
'Stole away.'"

This, with my aversion to leaping hedges, made me
withdraw to a rising ground, from whence I could
have the pleasure of the whole chase, without the
fatigue of keeping in with the hounds. The hare
immediately threw them above a mile behind her;
but I was pleased to find, that instead of running
straight forwards, or, in hunter's language, flying the
country, as I was afraid she might have done, she
wheeled about, and described a sort of circle round
the hill where I had taken my station, in such manner
as gave me a very distinct view of the sport. I could
see her first pass by, and the dogs some time afterwards unravelling the whole track she had made,
and following her through all her doubles. I was at

Stole away. The correct hunting cry which the Spectator
should have given.

the same time delighted in observing that deference which the rest of the pack paid to each particular hound, according to the character he had acquired amongst them: if they were at a fault, and an old hound of reputation opened but once, he was immediately followed by the whole cry; while a raw dog, or one who was a noted liar, might have yelped his heart out without being taken notice of.

The hare now, after having squatted two or three times, and been put up again as often, came still nearer to the place where she was at first started. The dogs pursued her, and these were followed by the jolly Knight, who rode upon a white gelding, encompassed by his tenants and servants, and cheering his hounds with all the gaiety of five and twenty. One of the sportsmen rode up to me, and told me that he was sure the chase was almost at an end, because the old dogs, which had hitherto lain behind, now headed the pack. The fellow was in the right. Our hare took a large field just under us, followed by the full cry in view. I must confess the brightness of the weather, the cheerfulness of everything around me, the chiding of the hounds, which was returned upon us in a double echo from two neighbouring hills, with the hallooing of the sportsmen and the sounding of the horn, lifted my spirits into a most lively pleasure, which I freely indulged because I knew it was innocent. If I was under any concern, it was on the account of the poor hare, that was now quite spent and almost within the reach of her enemies; when the huntsman, getting

Cheering his Hounds
with all the Gaiety of Five and Twenty.

forward, threw down his pole before the dogs. They
were now within eight yards of that game which
they had been pursuing for almost as many hours;
yet on the signal before mentioned they all made
a sudden stand, and though they continued opening
as much as before, durst not once attempt to pass
beyond the pole. At the same time Sir Roger rode
forward, and alighting, took up the hare in his arms;
which he soon delivered to one of his servants, with
an order, if she could be kept alive, to let her go in
his great orchard; where it seems he has several
of these prisoners of war, who live together in a
very comfortable captivity. I was highly pleased
to see the discipline of the pack, and the good nature
of the Knight, who could not find in his heart to
murder a creature that had given him so much
diversion.

As we were returning home, I remembered that
Monsieur Paschal in his most excellent discourse
on "the misery of man," tells us, that "all our
endeavours after greatness proceed from nothing
but a desire of being surrounded by a multitude of
persons and affairs that may hinder us from looking
into ourselves, which is a view we cannot bear." He
afterwards goes on to show that our love of sports
comes from the same reason, and is particularly
severe upon hunting. "What," says he, "unless
it be to drown thought, can make men throw away

Pole. A leaping-pole carried by the huntsman, who was on
foot, and thrown by him as a signal to the hounds to stop.
Monsieur Paschal. French philosopher: 1622–62.

so much time and pains upon a silly animal, which they might buy cheaper in the market? " The foregoing reflection is certainly just, when a man suffers his whole mind to be drawn into his sports, and altogether loses himself in the woods; but does not affect those who propose a far more laudable end for this exercise; I mean, the preservation of health, and keeping all the organs of the soul in a condition to execute her orders. Had that incomparable person, whom I last quoted, been a little more indulgent to himself in this point, the world might probably have enjoyed him much longer: whereas, through too great an application to his studies in his youth, he contracted that ill habit of body, which, after a tedious sickness, carried him off in the fortieth year of his age; and the whole history we have of his life till that time, is but one continued account of the behaviour of a noble soul struggling under innumerable pains and distempers.

For my own part, I intend to hunt twice a week during my stay with Sir Roger; and shall prescribe the moderate use of this exercise to all my country friends, as the best kind of physic for mending a bad constitution, and preserving a good one.

I cannot do this better, than in the following lines out of Mr. Dryden:—

> The first physicians by debauch were made;
> Excess began, and sloth sustains the trade.
> By chase our long-liv'd fathers earn'd their food;
> Toil strung the nerves, and purifi'd the blood;

Habit. Constitution.

But we their sons, a pamper'd race of men,
Are dwindled down to threescore years and ten.
Better to hunt in fields for health unbought,
Than fee the doctor for a nauseous draught.
The wise for cure on exercise depend;
God never made his work for man to mend.

X.

No. 117.　　　Saturday, July 14

Ipsi sibi somnia fingunt.

Virg. *Ecl.* viii. ver. 108.

Their own imaginations they deceive.

There are some opinions in which a man should stand neuter, without engaging his assent to one side or the other. Such a hovering faith as this, which refuses to settle upon any determination, is absolutely necessary in a mind that is careful to avoid errors and prepossessions. When the arguments press equally on both sides in matters that are indifferent to us, the safest method is to give up ourselves to neither.

It is with this temper of mind that I consider the subject of witchcraft. When I hear the relations that are made from all parts of the world, not only from Norway and Lapland, from the East and West Indies, but from every particular nation in Europe, I cannot forbear thinking that there is such an intercourse

Neuter. Neutral.　　　　*Engaging.* Binding.
Determination. Fixed opinion.

and commerce with evil spirits, as that which we
express by the name of witchcraft. But when I
consider that the ignorant and credulous parts of
the world abound most in these relations, and that
the persons among us, who are supposed to engage
in such an infernal commerce, are people of a weak
understanding and crazed imagination, and at the
same time reflect upon the many impostures and
delusions of this nature that have been detected
in all ages, I endeavour to suspend my belief till I
hear more certain accounts than any which have yet
come to my knowledge. In short, when I consider
the question whether there are such persons in the
world as those we call witches, my mind is divided
between the two opposite opinions; or rather, (to
speak my thoughts freely) I believe in general that
there is, and has been such a thing as witchcraft;
but, at the same time, can give no credit to any
particular instance of it.

I am engaged in this speculation by some occurrences that I met with yesterday, which I shall give
my reader an account of at large. As I was walking
with my friend Sir Roger by the side of one of his
woods, an old woman applied herself to me for my
charity. Her dress and figure put me in mind of the
following description in Otway:—

> In a close lane as I pursu'd my journey,
> I spy'd a wrinkled Hag, with age grown double,
> Picking dry sticks, and mumbling to herself.
> Her eyes with scalding rheum were gall'd and red;
> Cold palsy shook her head; her hands seem'd wither'd;
> And on her crooked shoulders had she wrapp'd

The tatter'd remnants of an old strip'd hanging,
Which serv'd to keep her carcase from the cold:
So there was nothing of a piece about her.
Her lower weeds were all o'er coarsely patch'd
With diff'rent-colour'd rags, black, red, white, yellow,
And seem'd to speak variety of wretchedness.

As I was musing on this description, and com-
paring it with the object before me, the Knight told
me, that this very old woman had the reputation
of a witch all over the country, that her lips were
observed to be always in motion, and that there was
not a switch about her house which her neighbours
did not believe had carried her several hundreds
of miles. If she chanced to stumble, they always
found sticks or straws that lay in the figure of a
cross before her. If she made any mistake at church,
and cried Amen in a wrong place, they never failed
to conclude that she was saying her prayers back-
wards. There was not a maid in the parish that
would take a pin of her, though she should offer
a bag of money with it. She goes by the name of
Moll White, and has made the country ring with
several imaginary exploits which are palmed upon
her. If the dairy-maid does not make the butter
come so soon as she would have it, Moll White is
at the bottom of the churn. If a horse sweats in
the stable, Moll White has been upon his back.
If a hare makes an unexpected escape from the
hounds, the huntsman curses Moll White. "Nay,"
(says Sir Roger) "I have known the master of the
pack, upon such an occasion, send one of his servants
to see if Moll White had been out that morning."

Moll White

This account raised my curiosity so far, that I begged my friend Sir Roger to go with me into her hovel, which stood in a solitary corner under the side of the wood. Upon our first entering Sir Roger winked to me, and pointed at something that stood behind the door, which, upon looking that way, I found to be an old broomstaff. At the same time he whispered me in the ear to take notice of a tabby cat that sat in the chimney-corner, which,

as the old Knight told me, lay under as bad a report
as Moll White herself; for, besides that Moll is said
often to accompany her in the same shape, the cat
is reported to have spoken twice or thrice in her
life, and to have played several pranks above the
capacity of an ordinary cat.

I was secretly concerned to see human nature
in so much wretchedness and disgrace, but at the
same time could not forbear smiling to hear Sir
Roger, who is a little puzzled about the old woman,
advising her as a justice of peace to avoid all com-
munication with the Devil, and never to hurt any
of her neighbour's cattle. We concluded our visit
with a bounty, which was very acceptable.

In our return home Sir Roger told me, that old
Moll had been often brought before him for making
children spit pins, and giving maids the nightmare;
and that the country people would be tossing her
into a pond, and trying experiments with her every
day, if it was not for him and his chaplain.

I have since found, upon inquiry, that Sir Roger
was several times staggered with the reports that
had been brought him concerning this old woman,
and would frequently have bound her over to the
county sessions, had not his chaplain with much ado
persuaded him to the contrary.

I have been the more particular in this account,
because I hear there is scarce a village in England
that has not a Moll White in it. When an old woman
begins to dote, and grow chargeable to a parish,

Been the more particular. Given fuller details.

she is generally turned into a witch, and fills the whole country with extravagant fancies, imaginary distempers, and terrifying dreams. In the meantime, the poor wretch that is the innocent occasion of so many evils begins to be frighted at herself, and sometimes confesses secret commerce and familiarities that her imagination forms in a delirious old age. This frequently cuts off charity from the greatest objects of compassion, and inspires people with a malevolence towards those poor decrepit parts of our species, in whom human nature is defaced by infirmity and dotage.   L.

No. 118.   MONDAY, JULY 16

Haeret lateri lethalis arundo.
VIRG. Æn. iv. ver. 73.

The fatal dart
Sticks in his side, and rankles in his heart.
DRYDEN.

THIS agreeable seat is surrounded with so many pleasing walks, which are struck out of a wood, in the midst of which the house stands, that one can hardly ever be weary of rambling from one labyrinth of delight to another. To one used to live in a city the charms of the country are so exquisite, that the mind is lost in a certain transport which raises us above ordinary life, and is yet not strong enough to be inconsistent with tranquillity.

Commerce. Intercourse.

This state of mind was I in, ravished with the murmur of waters, the whisper of breezes, the singing of birds; and whether I looked up to the heavens, down to the earth, or turned on the prospects around me, still struck with new sense of pleasure; when I found by the voice of my friend, who walked by me, that we had insensibly strolled into the grove sacred to the widow. "This woman," says he, "is of all others the most unintelligible; she either designs to marry, or she does not. What is the most perplexing of all, is, that she doth not either say to her lovers she has any resolution against that condition of life in general, or that she banishes them; but, conscious of her own merit, she permits their addresses, without fear of any ill consequence, or want of respect, from their rage or despair. She has that in her aspect, against which it is impossible to offend. A man whose thoughts are constantly bent upon so agreeable an object, must be excused if the ordinary occurrences in conversation are below his attention. I call her indeed perverse; but, alas! why do I call her so? Because her superior merit is such, that I cannot approach her without awe, that my heart is checked by too much esteem: I am angry that her charms are not more acceptable, that I am more inclined to worship than salute her: how often have I wished her unhappy, that I might have an opportunity of serving her? and how often troubled in that very imagination, at giving her the pain of being obliged? Well, I have

Conversation. General intercourse.　　　*Salute.* Kiss.

led a miserable life in secret upon her account; but fancy she would have condescended to have some regard for me, if it had not been for that watchful animal her confidant.

" Of all persons under the sun " (continued he, calling me by my name) " be sure to set a mark upon confidants: they are of all people the most impertinent. What is most pleasant to observe in them, is, that they assume to themselves the merit of the persons whom they have in their custody. Orestilla is a great fortune, and in wonderful danger of surprises, therefore full of suspicions of the least indifferent thing, particularly careful of new acquaintance, and of growing too familiar with the old. Themista, her favourite woman, is every whit as careful of whom she speaks to, and what she says. Let the ward be a beauty, her confidant shall treat you with an air of distance; let her be a fortune, and she assumes the suspicious behaviour of her friend and patroness. Thus it is that very many of our unmarried women of distinction, are to all intents and purposes married, except the consideration of different sexes. They are directly under the conduct of their whisperer, and think they are in a state of freedom, while they can prate with one of these attendants of all men in general, and still avoid the man they most like. You do not see one heiress in a hundred whose fate does not turn upon this circumstance of choosing a confidant. Thus it is

Pleasant. Ludicrous.
Except the consideration of. Except in respect of.

that the lady is addressed to, presented and flattered,
only by proxy, in her woman. In my case, how is it
possible that—" Sir Roger was proceeding in his
harangue, when we heard the voice of one speaking
very importunately, and repeating these words,
"What, not one smile?" We followed the sound
till we came to a close thicket, on the other side
of which we saw a young woman sitting as it were
in a personated sullenness, just over a transparent
fountain. Opposite to her stood Mr. William, Sir
Roger's master of the game. The Knight whispered
me, "Hist! these are lovers." The huntsman
looking earnestly at the shadow of the young maiden
in the stream, "Oh thou dear picture, if thou couldst
remain there in the absence of that fair creature
whom you represent in the water, how willingly
could I stand here satisfied for ever, without troubling
my dear Betty herself with any mention of her un-
fortunate William, whom she is angry with: but
alas! when she pleases to be gone, thou wilt also
vanish — yet let me talk to thee while thou dost
stay. Tell my dearest Betty thou dost not more
depend upon her, than does her William: her absence will make away with me as well as thee. If
she offers to remove thee, I will jump into these
waves to lay hold on thee; herself, her own dear
person, I must never embrace again.—Still do you

Presented. I.e., with gifts.
Personated sullenness. Pretended, or possibly the image
of, sullenness.
Master of the game. Huntsman.

hear me without one smile—It is too much to bear—"
He had no sooner spoke these words, but he made
an offer of throwing himself into the water: at which
his mistress started up, and at the next instant he
jumped across the fountain and met her in an embrace. She, half recovering from her fright, said, in
the most charming voice imaginable, and with a
tone of complaint, " I thought how well you would
drown yourself. No, no, you won't drown yourself
till you have taken your leave of Susan Holiday."
The huntsman, with a tenderness that spoke the most
passionate love, and with his cheek close to hers,
whispered the softest vows of fidelity in her ear,
and cried, " Don't, my dear, believe a word Kate
Willow says; she is spiteful, and makes stories
because she loves to hear me talk to herself for your
sake." " Look you there," quoth Sir Roger, " do
you see there, all mischief comes from confidants!
But let us not interrupt them; the maid is honest,
and the man dares not be otherwise, for he knows
I loved her father: I will interpose in this matter,
and hasten the wedding. Kate Willow is a witty
mischievous wench in the neighbourhood, who was
a beauty, and makes me hope I shall see the perverse widow in her condition. She was so flippant
with her answers to all the honest fellows that came
near her, and so very vain of her beauty, that she
has valued herself upon her charms till they are
ceased. She therefore now makes it her business
to prevent other young women from being more
discreet than she was herself: however, the saucy

thing said the other day well enough, ' Sir Roger and I must make a match, for we are both despised by those we loved.' The hussy has a great deal of power wherever she comes, and has her share of cunning.

" However, when I reflect upon this woman, I do not know whether in the main I am the worse for having loved her: whenever she is recalled to my imagination my youth returns, and I feel a forgotten warmth in my veins. This affliction in my life has streaked all my conduct with a softness, of which I should otherwise have been incapable. It is, perhaps, to this dear image in my heart owing that I am apt to relent, that I easily forgive, and that many desirable things are grown into my temper, which I should not have arrived at by better motives than the thought of being one day hers. I am pretty well satisfied such a passion as I have had is never well cured; and, between you and me, I am often apt to imagine it has had some whimsical effect upon my brain: for I frequently find, that in my most serious discourse I let fall some comical familiarity of speech, or odd phrase, that makes the company laugh; however, I cannot but allow she is a most excellent woman. When she is in the country I warrant she does not run into dairies, but reads upon the nature of plants; but has a glass-hive, and comes into the garden out of books to see them work, and observe the policies of their commonwealth. She

Whimsical. Fantastic.   *Upon.* About.
                Policies. Organisation.

understands everything. I would give ten pounds
to hear her argue with my friend Sir Andrew Freeport about trade. No, no, for all she looks so innocent
as it were, take my word for it she is no fool."   T.

No. 122.   FRIDAY, JULY 20

Comes jucundus in via pro vehiculo est.
                              PUBL. SYR. *Frag.*

An agreeable companion upon the road is as good as a
  coach.

A MAN'S first care should be to avoid the reproaches
of his own heart; his next, to escape the censures
of the world: if the last interferes with the former,
it ought to be entirely neglected; but otherwise
there cannot be a greater satisfaction to an honest
mind, than to see those approbations which it gives
itself seconded by the applauses of the public: a
man is more sure of his conduct, when the verdict
he passes upon his own behaviour is thus warranted
and confirmed by the opinion of all that know
him.

My worthy friend Sir Roger is one of those who is
not only at peace within himself, but beloved and
esteemed by all about him. He receives a suitable
tribute for his universal benevolence to mankind,
in the returns of affection and good-will, which are
paid him by every one that lives within his neighbourhood. I lately met with two or three odd instances of that general respect which is shown to

the good old Knight. He would needs carry Will Wimble and myself with him to the county assizes: as we were upon the road Will Wimble joined a couple of plain men who rid before us, and conversed with them for some time; during which my friend Sir Roger acquainted me with their characters.

"The first of them," says he, "that has a spaniel by his side, is a yeoman of about an hundred pounds a year, an honest man: he is just within the Game Act, and qualified to kill an hare or a pheasant: he knocks down a dinner with his gun twice or thrice a week; and by that means lives much cheaper than those who have not so good an estate as himself. He would be a good neighbour if he did not destroy so many partridges: in short, he is a very sensible man; shoots flying; and has been several times foreman of the petty jury.

"The other that rides along with him is Tom Touchy, a fellow famous for taking the law of everybody. There is not one in the town where he lives that he has not sued at the quarter sessions. The rogue had once the impudence to go to law with the widow. His head is full of costs, damages, and ejectments: he plagued a couple of honest gentlemen so long for a trespass in breaking one of his hedges, till he was forced to sell the ground it inclosed to defray the charges of the prosecution: his father left him fourscore pounds a year; but he has cast and been cast so often, that he is not now worth thirty. I

Game Act. See note on p. 19.
Cast and been cast. Won and lost his case.

suppose he is going upon the old business of the willow tree."

As Sir Roger was giving me this account of Tom Touchy, Will Wimble and his two companions stopped short till we came up to them. After having paid their respects to Sir Roger, Will told him that Mr. Touchy and he must appeal to him upon a dispute that arose between them. Will it seems had been giving his fellow-traveller an account of his angling one day in such a hole; when Tom Touchy, instead of hearing out his story, told him that Mr. Such-a-one, if he pleased, might take the law of him for fishing in that part of the river. My friend Sir Roger heard them both, upon a round trot; and after having

Upon a round trot. While trotting briskly.

paused some time told them, with the air of a man who would not give his judgment rashly, that much might be said on both sides. They were neither of them dissatisfied with the Knight's determination, because neither of them found himself in the wrong by it: upon which we made the best of our way to the assizes.

The court was sat before Sir Roger came; but notwithstanding all the justices had taken their places upon the bench, they made room for the old Knight at the head of them; who for his reputation in the county took occasion to whisper in the judge's ear, "That he was glad his Lordship had met with so much good weather in his circuit." I was listening to the proceeding of the court with much attention, and infinitely pleased with that great appearance and solemnity which so properly accompanies such a public administration of our laws; when, after about an hour's sitting, I observed to my great surprise, in the midst of a trial, that my friend Sir Roger was getting up to speak. I was in some pain for him, till I found he had acquitted himself of two or three sentences, with a look of much business and great intrepidity.

Upon his first rising the court was hushed, and a general whisper ran among the country people, that Sir Roger was up. The speech he made was so little to the purpose, that I shall not trouble my readers with an account of it; and I believe was not so much designed by the Knight himself to inform the court, as to give him a figure in my eye, and keep up his credit in the country.

I was highly delighted, when the court rose, to see the gentlemen of the country gathering about my old friend, and striving who should compliment him most; at the same time that the ordinary people gazed upon him at a distance, not a little admiring his courage, that was not afraid to speak to the judge.

In our return home we met with a very odd accident; which I cannot forbear relating, because it shows how desirous all who know Sir Roger are of giving him marks of their esteem. When we were arrived upon the verge of his estate, we stopped at a little inn to rest ourselves and our horses. The man of the house had it seems been formerly a servant in the Knight's family; and to do honour to his old master, had some time since, unknown to Sir Roger, put him up in a sign-post before the door; so that the Knight's head had hung out upon the road about a week before he himself knew anything of the matter. As soon as Sir Roger was acquainted with it, finding that his servant's indiscretion proceeded wholly from affection and good-will, he only told him that he had made him too high a compliment; and when the fellow seemed to think that could hardly be, added with a more decisive look, " That it was too great an honour for any man under a duke"; but told him at the same time that it might be altered with a very few touches, and that he himself would be at the charge of it. Accordingly they got a painter by the Knight's

Accident. Incident.　　　*Charge.* Expense.

directions to add a pair of whiskers to the face, and by a little aggravation of the features to change it into the Saracen's Head. I should not have known this story had not the innkeeper, upon Sir Roger's alighting, told him in my hearing, "That his honour's head was brought back last night with the alterations that he had ordered to be made in it." Upon this my friend, with his usual cheerfulness, related the particulars above mentioned, and ordered the head to be brought into the room. I could not forbear discovering greater expressions of mirth than ordinary upon the appearance of this monstrous face, under which, notwithstanding it was made to frown and stare in a most extraordinary manner, I could still discover a distant resemblance of my old friend. Sir Roger upon seeing me laugh, desired me to tell him truly if I thought it possible for people to know him in that disguise. I at first kept my usual silence; but upon the Knight's conjuring me to tell him whether it was not still more like himself than a Saracen, I composed my countenance in the best manner I could, and replied, that much might be said on both sides.

These several adventures, with the Knight's behaviour in them, gave me as pleasant a day as ever I met with in any of my travels. L.

Aggravation. Exaggeration.
Conjuring. Adjuring, entreating.

No. 130.   MONDAY, JULY 30

Semperque recentes
Convectare juvat praedas, et vivere rapto.
                    VIRG. Æn. vii. ver. 748.

Hunting their sport, and plund'ring was their trade.
                                    DRYDEN.

As I was yesterday riding out in the fields with my
friend Sir Roger, we saw at a little distance from us
a troop of gipsies. Upon the first discovery of them,
my friend was in some doubt whether he should not
exert the Justice of the Peace upon such a band of
lawless vagrants; but not having his clerk with him,
who is a necessary counsellor on these occasions,
and fearing that his poultry might fare the worse
for it, he let the thought drop: but at the same time
gave me a particular account of the mischiefs they do
in the country, in stealing people's goods and spoiling
their servants. " If a stray piece of linen hangs upon
an hedge," says Sir Roger, " they are sure to have
it; if the hog loses his way in the fields, it is ten to
one but he becomes their prey; our geese cannot
live in peace for them; if a man prosecutes them
with severity, his hen-roost is sure to pay for it:
they generally straggle into these parts about this
time of the year; and set the heads of our servant-
maids so agog for husbands, that we do not expect
to have any business done as it should be whilst
they are in the country. I have an honest dairy-

Exert. Exert the power of.

maid who crosses their hands with a piece of silver
every summer, and never fails being promised the
handsomest young fellow in the parish for her pains.
Your friend the butler has been fool enough to be
seduced by them; and though he is sure to lose a
knife, a fork, or a spoon every time his fortune is
told him, generally shuts himself up in the pantry
with an old gipsy for above half an hour once in a
twelvemonth. Sweethearts are the things they live
upon, which they bestow very plentifully upon all
those that apply themselves to them. You see now
and then some handsome young jades among them:
the sluts have very often white teeth and black
eyes."

Sir Roger observing that I listened with great
attention to his account of a people who were so
entirely new to me, told me, that if I would they
should tell us our fortunes. As I was very well
pleased with the Knight's proposal, we rid up and
communicated our hands to them. A Cassandra of
the crew, after having examined my lines very
diligently, told me, that I loved a pretty maid in a
corner, that I was a good woman's man, with some
other particulars which I do not think proper to
relate. My friend Sir Roger alighted from his horse,
and exposing his palm to two or three that stood by
him, they crumpled it into all shapes, and diligently
scanned every wrinkle that could be made in it;

Cassandra. Reference to the mad prophetess of that name
in the story of Troy.

In a corner. In secret.

"Told him, That he had a Widow in his Line of Life"

when one of them, who was older and more sunburnt than the rest, told him, that he had a widow in his line of life: upon which the Knight cried, "Go, go, you are an idle baggage"; and at the same time smiled upon me. The gipsy finding he was not displeased in his heart, told him, after a further inquiry into his hand, that his true-love was constant, and that she should dream of him to-night: my old friend cried "pish," and bid her go on. The gipsy told him that he was a bachelor, but would not be so long; and that he was dearer to somebody than he thought: the Knight still repeated she was an idle baggage, and bid her go on. "Ah, master," says the gipsy, "that roguish leer of yours makes a pretty woman's heart ache; you ha'n't that simper about the mouth for nothing—" The uncouth gibberish with which all this was uttered, like the darkness of an oracle, made us the more attentive to it. To be short, the Knight left the money with her that he had crossed her hand with, and got up again on his horse.

As we were riding away, Sir Roger told me, that he knew several sensible people who believed these gipsies now and then foretold very strange things; and for half an hour together appeared more jocund than ordinary. In the height of his good-humour, meeting a common beggar upon the road who was no conjurer, as he went to relieve him he found his pocket was picked; that being a kind of palmistry at which this race of vermin are very dexterous.

I might here entertain my reader with historical remarks on this idle profligate people, who infest all the countries of Europe, and live in the midst of governments in a kind of commonwealth by themselves. But instead of entering into observations of this nature, I shall fill the remaining part of my paper with a story which is still fresh in Holland,

and was printed in one of our monthly accounts about twenty years ago. "As the *trekschuyt,* or hackney-boat, which carries passengers from Leyden to Amsterdam, was putting off, a boy running along the side of the canal desired to be taken in; which the master of the boat refused, because the lad had not quite money enough to pay the usual fare. An eminent merchant being pleased with the looks of the boy, and secretly touched with compassion towards him, paid the money for him, and ordered him to be taken on board. Upon talking with him afterwards, he found that he could speak readily in three or four languages, and learned upon further examination that he had been stolen away when he was a child by a gipsy, and had rambled ever since with a gang of those strollers up and down several parts of Europe. It happened that the merchant, whose heart seems to have inclined towards the boy by a secret kind of instinct, had himself lost a child some years before. The parents, after a long search for him, gave him for drowned in one of the canals with which that country abounds; and the mother was so afflicted at the loss of a fine boy, who was her only son, that she died for grief of it. Upon laying together all particulars, and examining the several moles and marks by which the mother used to describe the child when he was first missing, the boy proved to be the son of the merchant whose heart had so unaccountably melted at the sight of him. The lad was very well pleased to find a father who was so

Strollers. Vagabonds.

D

rich, and likely to leave him a good estate; the father
on the other hand was not a little delighted to see
a son return to him, whom he had given for lost, with
such a strength of constitution, sharpness of understanding, and skill in languages." Here the printed
story leaves off; but if I may give credit to reports,
our linguist having received such extraordinary rudi-
ments towards a good education, was afterwards
trained up in everything that becomes a gentleman;
wearing off by little and little all the vicious habits
and practices that he had been used to in the course
of his peregrinations: nay, it is said, that he has
since been employed in foreign courts upon national
business, with great reputation to himself and honour
to those who sent him, and that he has visited several
countries as a public minister, in which he formerly
wandered as a gipsy.   C.

No. 131   TUESDAY, JULY 31

Ipsae rursum concedite sylvae.
                            VIRG. *Ecl.* x. ver. 63.

Once more, ye woods, adieu.

IT is usual for a man who loves country sports to
preserve the game on his own grounds, and divert
himself upon those that belong to his neighbour.
My friend Sir Roger generally goes two or three
miles from his house, and gets into the frontiers
of his estate, before he beats about in search of a

hare or partridge, on purpose to spare his own fields,
where he is always sure of finding diversion, when
the worst comes to the worst. By this means the
breed about his house has time to increase and
multiply, beside that the sport is the more agreeable
where the game is the harder to come at, and where
it does not lie so thick as to produce any perplexity
or confusion in the pursuit. For these reasons the
country gentleman, like the fox, seldom preys near
his own home.

In the same manner I have made a month's
excursion out of the town, which is the great field
of game for sportsmen of my species, to try my
fortune in the country, where I have started several
subjects, and hunted them down, with some pleasure
to myself, and I hope to others. I am here forced
to use a great deal of diligence before I can spring
anything to my mind, whereas in town, whilst I
am following one character, it is ten to one but I
am crossed in my way by another, and put up such
a variety of odd creatures in both sexes, that they
foil the scent of one another, and puzzle the chase.
My greatest difficulty in the country is to find sport,
and in town to choose it. In the meantime, as I
have given a whole month's rest to the cities of
London and Westminster, I promise myself abun-
dance of new game upon my return thither.

It is indeed high time for me to leave the country,
since I find the whole neighbourhood begin to grow
very inquisitive after my name and character: my

Spring. Start from its hiding-place.

love of solitude, taciturnity, and particular way of life, having raised a great curiosity in all these parts.

The notions which have been framed of me are various: some look upon me as very proud, some as very modest, and some as very melancholy. Will Wimble, as my friend the butler tells me, observing me very much alone, and extremely silent when I am in company, is afraid I have killed a man. The country people seem to suspect me for a conjurer; and some of them, hearing of the visit which I made to Moll White, will needs have it that Sir Roger has brought down a cunning man with him, to cure the old woman, and free the country from her charms. So that the character which I go under in part of the neighbourhood, is what they here call a "white witch."

A justice of peace, who lives about five miles off, and is not of Sir Roger's party, has it seems said twice or thrice at his table, that he wishes Sir Roger does not harbour a Jesuit in his house, and that he thinks the gentlemen of the country would do very well to make me give some account of myself.

On the other side, some of Sir Roger's friends are afraid the old Knight is imposed upon by a designing fellow, and as they have heard that he converses very promiscuously when he is in town, do not know but he has brought down with him

Particular. Peculiar.

White witch. One who uses supernatural powers, but only for good purposes.

Converses very promiscuously. Mixes with all sorts of people.

some discarded Whig, that is sullen, and says nothing
because he is out of place.

Such is the variety of opinions which are here
entertained of me, so that I pass among some for a
disaffected person, and among others for a Popish
priest; among some for a wizard, and among others
for a murderer; and all this for no other reason,
that I can imagine, but because I do not hoot and
hollow, and make a noise. It is true my friend Sir
Roger tells them, *That it is my way*, and that I am
only a philosopher; but this will not satisfy them.
They think there is more in me than he discovers,
and that I do not hold my tongue for nothing.

For these and other reasons I shall set out for
London to-morrow, having found by experience that
the country is not a place for a person of my temper,
who does not love jollity, and what they call good
neighbourhood. A man that is out of humour when
an unexpected guest breaks in upon him, and does
not care for sacrificing an afternoon to every chance-
comer; that will be the master of his own time,
and the pursuer of his own inclinations, makes but
a very unsociable figure in this kind of life. I shall
therefore retire into the town, if I may make use of
that phrase, and get into the crowd again as fast
as I can, in order to be alone. I can there raise what
speculations I please upon others, without being
observed myself, and at the same time enjoy all
the advantages of company with all the privileges

Discarded. Out of office.   *Discovers.* Reveals.
          Neighbourhood. Sociability.

of solitude. In the meanwhile, to finish the month, and conclude these my rural speculations, I shall here insert a letter from my friend Will Honeycomb, who has not lived a month for these forty years out of the smoke of London, and rallies me after his way upon my country life.

DEAR SPEC,

I suppose this letter will find thee picking of daisies, or smelling to a lock of hay, or passing away thy time in some innocent country diversion of the like nature. I have however orders from the club to summon thee up to town, being all of us cursedly afraid thou wilt not be able to relish our company, after thy conversations with Moll White and Will Wimble. Prithee do not send us up any more stories of a cock and a bull, nor frighten the town with spirits and witches. Thy speculations begin to smell confoundedly of woods and meadows. If thou dost not come up quickly, we shall conclude that thou art in love with one of Sir Roger's dairymaids. Service to the Knight. Sir Andrew is grown the cock of the club since he left us, and if he does not return quickly will make every mother's son of us commonwealth's men.

Dear Spec,
Thine eternally,
WILL HONEYCOMB.

C.

Thee. The now obsolete familiar use of *thou* and *thee.*
Commonwealth's men. Republicans.

No. 269.   TUESDAY, JANUARY 8

> *Aevo rarissima nostro*
> *Simplicitas.*
>
> OVID, *Ars Am.* lib. i. ver. 241.

Most rare is now our old simplicity.

DRYDEN.

I WAS this morning surprised with a great knocking at the door, when my landlady's daughter came up to me, and told me that there was a man below desired to speak with me. Upon my asking her who it was, she told me it was a very grave elderly person, but that she did not know his name. I immediately went down to him, and found him to be the coachman of my worthy friend Sir Roger de Coverley. He told me, that his master came to town last night, and would be glad to take a turn with me in Gray's Inn walks. As I was wondering in myself what had brought Sir Roger to town, not having lately received any letter from him, he told me that his master was come up to get a sight of Prince Eugene, and that he desired I would immediately meet him.

I was not a little pleased with the curiosity of the old Knight, though I did not much wonder at it, having heard him say more than once in private discourse, that he looked upon Prince Eugenio (for

Turn. Stroll.

Prince Eugene. Prince of Savoy (1663–1736), who aided Marlborough at Blenheim and elsewhere, and was at this time on a visit to London.

so the Knight always calls him) to be a greater man than Scanderbeg.

I was no sooner come into Gray's Inn walks, but I heard my friend upon the terrace hemming twice or thrice to himself with great vigour, for he loves to clear his pipes in good air (to make use of his own phrase), and is not a little pleased with any one who takes notice of the strength which he still exerts in his morning hems.

I was touched with a secret joy at the sight of the good old man, who before he saw me was engaged in conversation with a beggar man that had asked an alms of him. I could hear my friend chide him for not finding out some work; but at the same time saw him put his hand in his pocket and give him sixpence.

Our salutations were very hearty on both sides, consisting of many kind shakes of the hand, and several affectionate looks which we cast upon one another. After which the Knight told me my good friend his chaplain was very well, and much at my service, and that the Sunday before he had made a most incomparable sermon out of Dr. Barrow. "I have left," says he, "all my affairs in his hands, and being willing to lay an obligation upon him, have deposited with him thirty merks, to be distributed among his poor parishioners."

Scanderbeg. George Castriota, a famous Albanian leader against the Turks (1403–68).

Hemming. Clearing his throat.

Merks. A merk is 13s. 4d., but only as a measure of value, not an actual coin. Compare our present use of a guinea.

He then proceeded to acquaint me with the welfare of Will Wimble. Upon which he put his hand into his fob, and presented me in his name with a tobacco-stopper, telling me that Will had been busy all the beginning of the winter in turning great quantities of them; and that he made a present of one to every gentleman in the country who has good principles, and smokes. He added, that poor Will was at present under great tribulation, for that Tom Touchy had taken the law of him for cutting some hazel-sticks out of one of his hedges.

Among other pieces of news which the Knight brought from his country seat, he informed me that Moll White was dead; and that about a month after her death the wind was so very high, that it blew down the end of one of his barns. " But for my own part," says Sir Roger, " I do not think that the old woman had any hand in it."

He afterwards fell into an account of the diversions which had passed in his house during the holidays; for Sir Roger, after the laudable custom of his ancestors, always keeps open house at Christmas. I learned from him that he had killed eight fat hogs for this season, that he had dealt about his chines very liberally amongst his neighbours, and that in particular he had sent a string of hogs-puddings with a pack of cards to every poor family in the parish. " I have often thought," says Sir Roger, " it happens very well that Christmas should fall out in the middle of winter. It is the most dead

Fob. Small pocket.

*D

uncomfortable time of the year, when the poor people would suffer very much from their poverty and cold, if they had not good cheer, warm fires, and Christmas gambols to support them. I love to rejoice their poor hearts at this season, and to see the whole village merry in my great hall. I allow a double quantity of malt to my small beer, and set it a running for twelve days to every one that calls for it. I have always a piece of cold beef and a mince-pie upon the table, and am wonderfully pleased to see my tenants pass away a whole evening in playing their innocent tricks, and smutting one another. Our friend Will Wimble is as merry as any of them, and shows a thousand roguish tricks upon these occasions."

I was very much delighted with the reflection of my old friend, which carried so much goodness in it. He then launched out into the praise of the late Act of Parliament for securing the Church of England, and told me, with great satisfaction, that he believed it already began to take effect, for that a rigid dissenter who chanced to dine at his house on Christmas Day, had been observed to eat very plentifully of his plum-porridge.

After having dispatched all our country matters, Sir Roger made several inquiries concerning the club, and particularly of his old antagonist Sir Andrew

Smutting one another. Blacking one another's faces in sport.

Act of Parliament. Act of Occasional Uniformity, 1710.

Rigid dissenter . . . plum-porridge. Many Puritans refused to observe Christmas Day, regarding it as smacking of Popery.

Freeport. He asked me with a kind of a smile, whether Sir Andrew had not taken the advantage of his absence, to vent among them some of his republican doctrines; but soon after gathering up his countenance into a more than ordinary seriousness, " Tell me truly," says he, " do not you think Sir Andrew had a hand in the Pope's procession? "— but without giving me time to answer him, " Well, well," says he, " I know you are a wary man, and do not care to talk of public matters."

The Knight then asked me if I had seen Prince Eugenio, and made me promise to get him a stand in some convenient place, where he might have a full sight of that extraordinary man, whose presence does so much honour to the British nation. He dwelt very long on the praises of this great general, and I found that, since I was with him in the country, he had drawn many just observations together out of his reading in Baker's *Chronicle*, and other authors, who always lie in his hall window, which very much redound to the honour of this prince.

Having passed away the greatest part of the morning in hearing the Knight's reflections, which were partly private, and partly political, he asked me if I would smoke a pipe with him over a dish of coffee at Squire's. As I love the old man, I take delight in complying with everything that is agreeable to him, and accordingly waited on him to the

Pope's procession. An annual Whig demonstration.
Baker's Chronicle. Chronicle of the Kings of England (1643), by Sir Richard Baker.
Waited on. Accompanied.

coffee-house, where his venerable figure drew upon us the eyes of the whole room. He had no sooner seated himself at the upper end of the high table, but he called for a clean pipe, a paper of tobacco, a dish of coffee, a wax-candle, and the *Supplement*, with such an air of cheerfulness and good humour, that all the boys in the coffee-room (who seemed to take pleasure in serving him) were at once employed on his several errands, insomuch that nobody else could come at a dish of tea, until the Knight had got all his conveniences about him.   L.

No. 329.   TUESDAY, MARCH 18

Ire tamen restat, Numa quo devenit, et Ancus.
              HOR. *Ep.* vi. l. i. ver. 27.

With Ancus, and with Numa, kings of Rome,
We must descend into the silent tomb.

MY friend Sir Roger de Coverley told me the other night, that he had been reading my paper upon Westminster Abbey, " in which," says he, " there are a great many ingenious fancies." He told me at the same time, that he observed I had promised another paper upon the Tombs, and that he should be glad to go and see them with me, not having visited them since he had read history. I could not at first imagine how this came into the Knight's head, till I recollected that he had been very busy

Bovs. Waiters.

all last summer upon Baker's *Chronicle*, which he has quoted several times in his disputes with Sir Andrew Freeport since his last coming to town. Accordingly I promised to call upon him the next morning, that we might go together to the Abbey.

I found the Knight under his butler's hands, who always shaves him. He was no sooner dressed than he called for a glass of the widow Trueby's water, which they told me he always drank before he went abroad. He recommended to me a dram of it at the same time, with so much heartiness, that I could not forbear drinking it. As soon as I had got it down, I found it very unpalatable, upon which the Knight observing that I had made several wry faces, told me that he knew I should not like it at first, but that it was the best thing in the world against the stone or gravel.

I could have wished indeed that he had acquainted me with the virtues of it sooner; but it was too late to complain, and I knew what he had done was out of goodwill. Sir Roger told me further, that he looked upon it to be very good for a man whilst he stayed in town, to keep off infection, and that he got together a quantity of it upon the first news of the sickness being at Dantzick: when of a sudden, turning short to one of his servants who stood behind him, he bid him call a hackney-coach, and take care it was an elderly man that drove it.

He then resumed his discourse upon Mrs. Trueby's water, telling me that the widow Trueby was one who did more good than all the doctors or apothecaries in the country: that she distilled every poppy that grew within five miles of her ; that she distributed her water gratis among all sorts of people; to which the Knight added, that she had a very great jointure, and that the whole country would fain have it a match between him and her; " and truly," says Sir Roger, " if I had not been engaged, perhaps I could not have done better."

His discourse was broken off by his man's telling him he had called a coach. Upon our going to it, after having cast his eye upon the wheels, he asked the coachman if his axle-tree was good; upon the fellow's telling him he would warrant it, the Knight turned to me, told me he looked like an honest man, and went in without further ceremony.

We had not gone far, when Sir Roger, popping out his head, called the coachman down from his box, and, upon presenting himself at the window, asked him if he smoked; as I was considering what this would end in, he bid him stop by the way at any good tobacconist's and take in a roll of their best Virginia. Nothing material happened in the remaining part of our journey, till we were set down at the west end of the Abbey.

As we went up the body of the church, the Knight pointed at the trophies upon one of the new monuments, and cried out, " A brave man, I warrant him!" Passing afterwards by Sir Cloudesley Shovel,

Jointure. Settlement.
Engaged. Pledged.
Sir Cloudesley Shovel. Admiral Sir Cloudesley Shovel, drowned off the Scilly Isles, 1707.

he flung his hand that way, and cried, " Sir Cloudesley Shovel! a very gallant man! " As he stood before Busby's tomb, the Knight uttered himself again after the same manner, " Dr. Busby, a great man! he whipped my grandfather; a very great man! I should have gone to him myself, if I had not been a blockhead; a very great man! "

We were immediately conducted to the little chapel on the right hand. Sir Roger, planting himself at our historian's elbow, was very attentive to everything he said, particularly to the account he gave us of the lord who had cut off the King of Morocco's head. Among several other figures, he was very well pleased to see the statesman Cecil upon his knees; and concluding them all to be great men, was conducted to the figure which represents that martyr to good housewifery, who died by the prick of a needle. Upon our interpreter's telling us that she was a maid of honour to Queen Elizabeth, the Knight was very inquisitive into her name and family; and after having regarded her finger for some time, " I wonder," says he, " that Sir Richard Baker has said nothing of her in his *Chronicle*."

We were then conveyed to the two coronation chairs, where my old friend after having heard that the stone underneath the most ancient of them, which was brought from Scotland, was called " Jacob's pillar," sat himself down in the chair;

Dr. Busby. The famous flogging headmaster of Westminster.

Cecil. Lord Burleigh, Queen Elizabeth's Lord High Treasurer.

and looking like the figure of an old Gothic king, asked our interpreter, what authority they had to say that Jacob had ever been in Scotland? The fellow, instead of returning him an answer, told him, that he hoped his honour would pay his forfeit. I could observe Sir Roger a little ruffled upon being thus trepanned; but our guide not insisting upon his demand, the Knight soon recovered his good humour, and whispered in my ear, that if Will Wimble were with us, and saw those two chairs, it would go hard but he would get a tobacco-stopper out of one or the other of them.

Sir Roger, in the next place, laid his hand upon Edward the Third's sword, and leaning upon the pommel of it, gave us the whole history of the Black Prince; concluding, that, in Sir Richard Baker's opinion, Edward the Third was one of the greatest princes that ever sat upon the English throne.

We were then shown Edward the Confessor's tomb; upon which Sir Roger acquainted us, that he was the first who touched for the evil; and afterwards Henry the Fourth's, upon which he shook his head, and told us there was fine reading in the casualties of that reign.

Our conductor then pointed to that monument where there is the figure of one of our English kings without an head; and upon giving us to know, that

Forfeit. Gratuity due for sitting in the chair.
Pommel. Part of the hilt.
Touched for the evil. The royal touch was regarded as a cure for scrofula as late as Queen Anne's time.
Casualties. Incidents.

the head, which was of beaten silver, had been stolen away several years since: " Some Whig, I'll warrant you," says Sir Roger; " you ought to lock up your kings better; they will carry off the body too, if you don't take care."

The glorious names of Henry the Fifth and Queen Elizabeth gave the Knight great opportunities of shining, and of doing justice to Sir Richard Baker; who, as our Knight observed with some surprise, had a great many kings in him, whose monuments he had not seen in the Abbey.

For my own part, I could not but be pleased to see the Knight show such an honest passion for the glory of his country, and such a respectful gratitude to the memory of its princes.

I must not omit, that the benevolence of my good old friend, which flows out towards every one he converses with, made him very kind to our inter-preter, whom he looked upon as an extraordinary man; for which reason he shook him by the hand at parting, telling him, that he should be very glad to see him at his lodgings in Norfolk Buildings, and talk over these matters with him more at leisure.

L.

No. 335.   TUESDAY, MARCH 25

Respicere exemplar vitae morumque jubebo
Doctum imitatorem, et veras hinc ducere voces.
                              HOR. *Ars Poet.* ver. 317.

Those are the likest copies, which are drawn
From the original of human life.
                                   ROSCOMMON.

MY friend Sir Roger de Coverley, when we last met
together at the club, told me that he had a great
mind to see the new tragedy with me, assuring me
at the same time, that he had not been at a play
these twenty years. "The last I saw," said Sir
Roger, "was the *Committee*, which I should not
have gone to neither, had not I been told beforehand that it was a good Church of England comedy."
He then proceeded to inquire of me who this Distressed Mother was; and upon hearing that she
was Hector's widow, he told me that her husband
was a brave man, and that when he was a schoolboy
he had read his life at the end of the dictionary.
My friend asked me, in the next place, if there would
not be some danger in coming home late, in case the
Mohocks should be abroad. "I assure you," says
he, "I thought I had fallen into their hands last
night; for I observed two or three lusty black men
that followed me half-way up Fleet Street, and

New tragedy. The Distressed Mother, by Ambrose Phillips.
Mohocks. Gangs of rowdies who roamed the streets at
night and assaulted passers-by. See *Spectator*, No. 324.

mended their pace behind me, in proportion as I put on to get away from them. You must know," continued the Knight with a smile, "I fancied they had a mind to *hunt* me; for I remember an honest gentleman in my neighbourhood, who was served such a trick in King Charles the Second's time, for which reason he has not ventured himself in town ever since. I might have shown them very good sport, had this been their design; for as I am an old fox-hunter, I should have turned and dodged, and have played them a thousand tricks they had never seen in their lives before." Sir Roger added, that if these gentlemen had any such intention, they did not succeed very well in it; "for I threw them out," says he, "at the end of Norfolk Street, where I doubled the corner, and got shelter in my lodgings before they could imagine what was become of me. However," says the Knight, "if Captain Sentry will make one with us to-morrow night, and if you will both of you call upon me about four o'clock, that we may be at the house before it is full, I will have my coach in readiness to attend you, for John tells me he has got the fore-wheels mended."

The Captain, who did not fail to meet me there at the appointed hour, bid Sir Roger fear nothing, for that he had put on the same sword which he made use of at the battle of Steenkirk. Sir Roger's servants, and among the rest my old friend the butler, had, I found, provided themselves with good

Put on. Put on speed.

oaken plants, to attend their master upon this occasion. When we had placed him in his coach, with myself at his left hand, the Captain before him, and his butler at the head of his footmen in the rear, we conveyed him in safety to the play-house, where after having marched up the entry in good order, the Captain and I went in with him, and seated him betwixt us in the pit. As soon as the house was full, and the candles lighted, my old friend stood up and looked about him with that pleasure, which a mind seasoned with humanity naturally feels in itself, at the sight of a multitude of people who seemed pleased with one another, and partake of the same common entertainment. I could not but fancy to myself, as the old man stood up in the middle of the pit, that he made a very proper centre to a tragic audience. Upon the entering of Pyrrhus, the Knight told me that he did not believe the King of France himself had a better strut. I was indeed very attentive to my old friend's remarks, because I looked upon them as a piece of natural criticism, and was well pleased to hear him, at the conclusion of almost every scene, telling me that he could not imagine how the play would end. One while he appeared much concerned for Andromache; and a little while after as much for Hermione; and was extremely puzzled to think what would become of Pyrrhus.

Seasoned with humanity. Tempered with kindliness.
Pyrrhus. Son of Achilles, to whom Hector's widow, Andromache, had fallen as his share of the plunder of Troy.

When Sir Roger saw Andromache's obstinate refusal to her lover's importunities, he whispered me in the ear, that he was sure she would never have him; to which he added, with a more than ordinary vehemence, " You cannot imagine, sir, what it is to have to do with a widow." Upon Pyrrhus his threatening afterwards to leave her, the Knight shook his head and muttered to himself, " Ay, do if you can." This part dwelt so much upon my friend's imagination, that at the close of the third act, as I was thinking of something else, he whispered me in the ear, " These widows, sir, are the most perverse creatures in the world. But pray," says he, " you that are a critic, is the play according to your dramatic rules, as you call them? Should your people in tragedy always talk to be understood? Why, there is not a single sentence in this play that I do not know the meaning of."

The fourth act very luckily begun before I had time to give the old gentleman an answer: " Well," says the Knight, sitting down with great satisfaction, " I suppose we are now to see Hector's ghost." He then renewed his attention, and, from time to time, fell a praising the widow. He made, indeed, a little mistake as to one of her pages, whom at his first entering he took for Astyanax; but quickly set himself right in that particular, though, at the same time, he owned he should have been very glad

Pyrrhus his. This use is due to a wrong idea that the possessive termination is an abbreviation of *his.*

Astyanax. Son of Hector and Andromache (and subject of one of the most touching passages in Homer).

to have seen the little boy, "who," says he, "must needs be a very fine child by the account that is given of him." Upon Hermione's going off with a menace to Pyrrhus, the audience gave a loud clap, to which Sir Roger added, "On my word, a notable young baggage!"

As there was a very remarkable silence and stillness in the audience during the whole action, it was natural for them to take the opportunity of the intervals between the acts, to express their opinion of the players, and of their respective parts. Sir Roger hearing a cluster of them praise Orestes, struck in with them, and told them, that he thought his friend Pylades was a very sensible man; as they were afterwards applauding Pyrrhus, Sir Roger put in a second time: "And let me tell you," says he, "though he speaks but little, I like the old fellow in whiskers as well as any of them." Captain Sentry seeing two or three wags, who sat near us, lean with an attentive ear towards Sir Roger, and fearing lest they should smoke the Knight, plucked him by the elbow, and whispered something in his ear, that lasted till the opening of the fifth act. The Knight was wonderfully attentive to the account which Orestes gives of Pyrrhus his death, and at the conclusion of it, told me it was such a bloody piece of work, that he was glad it was not done upon the stage. Seeing afterwards Orestes in his raving fit, he grew more than ordinary serious, and took occasion to moralise (in his way) upon an evil conscience,

Smoke. A slang word, equivalent to the modern *rag.*

adding, that *Orestes, in his madness, looked as if he saw something.*

As we were the first that came into the house, so we were the last that went out of it; being resolved to have a clear passage for our old friend, whom we did not care to venture among the justling of the crowd. Sir Roger went out fully satisfied with his entertainment, and we guarded him to his lodging in he same manner that we brought him to the play-house; being highly pleased, for my own part, not only with the performance of the excellent piece which had been presented, but with the satisfaction which it had given to the old man.   L.

No. 383.   TUESDAY, MAY 20

Criminibus debent hortos.

JUV. *Sat.* i. ver. 75.

A beauteous garden, but by vice maintain'd.

As I was sitting in my chamber and thinking on a subject for my next *Spectator*, I heard two or three irregular bounces at my landlady's door, and upon the opening of it, a loud cheerful voice inquiring whether the Philosopher was at home. The child who went to the door answered very innocently, that he did not lodge there. I immediately re-collected that it was my good friend Sir Roger's

Bounces. Loud knocks.
Recollected. We should now say *recognised.*

voice; and that I had promised to go with him on the water to Spring Garden, in case it proved a good evening. The Knight put me in mind of my promise from the bottom of the staircase, but told me that if I was speculating he would stay below till I had done. Upon my coming down I found all the children of the family got about my old friend, and my landlady herself, who is a notable prating gossip, engaged in a conference with him; being mightily pleased with his stroking her little boy upon the head, and bidding him be a good child, and mind his book.

We were no sooner come to the Temple stairs, but we were surrounded with a crowd of watermen offering us their respective services. Sir Roger, after having looked about him very attentively, spied one with a wooden leg, and immediately gave him orders to get his boat ready. As we were walking towards it, "You must know," says Sir Roger, "I never make use of anybody to row me, that has not either lost a leg or an arm. I would rather bate him a few strokes of his oar than not employ an honest man that has been wounded in the Queen's service. If I was a lord or a bishop, and kept a barge, I would not put a fellow in my livery that had not a wooden leg."

My old friend, after having seated himself, and trimmed the boat with his coachman, who, being

Spring Garden. At Vauxhall.
Speculating. Ruminating.
Bate him a few strokes of his oar. Excuse his rowing slowly.
Trimmed. Balanced.

I found all the Children of the Family got about my old Friend

a very sober man, always serves for ballast on these occasions, we made the best of our way for Fox-Hall. Sir Roger obliged the waterman to give us the history of his right leg, and hearing that he had left it at La Hogue, with many particulars which passed in that glorious action, the Knight in the triumph of his heart made several reflections on the greatness of the British nation; as, that one Englishman could beat three Frenchmen; that we could never be in danger of popery so long as we took care of our fleet; that the Thames was the noblest river in Europe, that London Bridge was a greater piece of work than any of the seven wonders of the world; with many other honest prejudices which naturally cleave to the heart of a true Englishman.

After some short pause, the old Knight turning about his head twice or thrice, to take a survey of this great metropolis, bid me observe how thick the city was set with churches, and that there was scarce a single steeple on this side Temple Bar. "A most heathenish sight!" says Sir Roger: "there is no religion at this end of the town. The fifty new churches will very much mend the prospect; but church work is slow, church work is slow!"

I do not remember I have anywhere mentioned in Sir Roger's character, his custom of saluting everybody that passes by him with a good-morrow or a good-night. This the old man does out of the overflowings of his humanity, though at the same time it renders him so popular among all his country neighbours, that it is thought to have gone a good way in making him once or twice knight of the shire. He cannot forbear this exercise of benevolence

---

The fifty new churches. Voted by Parliament in 1711 for the western suburbs.

Knight of the shire. M.P. See p. 44.

even in town, when he meets with any one in his morning or evening walk. It broke from him to several boats that passed by us upon the water; but to the Knight's great surprise, as he gave the good-night to two or three young fellows a little before our landing, one of them, instead of returning the civility, asked us, what queer old put we had in the boat? with a great deal of the like Thames ribaldry. Sir Roger seemed a little shocked at first, but at length assuming a face of magistracy, told us, " That if he were a Middlesex justice, he would make such vagrants know that her Majesty's subjects were no more to be abused by water than by land."

We were now arrived at Spring Garden, which is exquisitely pleasant at this time of the year. When I considered the fragrancy of the walks and bowers, with the choirs of birds that sung upon the trees, and the loose tribe of people that walked under their shades, I could not but look upon the place as a kind of Mahometan paradise. Sir Roger told me it put him in mind of a little coppice by his house in the country, which his chaplain used to call an aviary of nightingales. " You must understand," says the Knight, " there is nothing in the world that pleases a man in love so much as your nightingale. Ah, Mr. Spectator! the many moonlight nights that I have walked by myself, and thought on the widow by the music of the nightingale! " He here fetched a deep sigh, and was falling into a fit of

Put. Rustic, boor.

musing, when a mask, who came behind him, gave him a gentle tap upon the shoulder, and asked him if he would drink a bottle of mead with her? But the Knight, being startled at so unexpected a familiarity, and displeased to be interrupted in his thoughts of the widow, told her, "she was a wanton baggage," and bid her go about her business.

We concluded our walk with a glass of Burton ale, and a slice of hung beef. When we had done eating ourselves, the Knight called a waiter to him, and bid him carry the remainder to the waterman that had but one leg. I perceived the fellow stared upon him at the oddness of the message, and was going to be saucy; upon which I ratified the Knight's commands with a peremptory look.   I.

No. 517   THURSDAY, OCTOBER 23

Heu pietas ! heu prisca fides !
                    VIRG. *Æn.* vi. ver. 878.

Mirror of ancient faith!
Undaunted worth! Inviolable truth!
                    DRYDEN.

WE last night received a piece of ill news at our club, which very sensibly afflicted every one of us. I question not but my readers themselves will be troubled at the hearing of it. To keep them no

Hung. Salted or spiced.   *Sensibly.* Keenly.

longer in suspense, Sir Roger de Coverley *is dead*.
He departed this life at his house in the country,
after a few weeks' sickness. Sir Andrew Freeport
has a letter from one of his correspondents in those
parts, that informs him the old man caught a cold
at the country sessions, as he was very warmly
promoting an address of his own penning, in which
he succeeded according to his wishes. But this
particular comes from a Whig justice of peace, who
was always Sir Roger's enemy and antagonist. I
have letters both from the chaplain and Captain
Sentry, which mention nothing of it, but are filled
with many particulars to the honour of the good old
man. I have likewise a letter from the butler, who
took so much care of me last summer when I was at
the Knight's house. As my friend the butler men-
tions, in the simplicity of his heart, several circumstances the others have passed over in silence, I
shall give my reader a copy of his letter, without
any alteration or diminution.

HONOURED SIR,
  Knowing that you was my old master's good friend,
I could not forbear sending you the melancholy news
of his death, which has afflicted the whole country, as
well as his poor servants, who loved him, I may say,
better than we did our lives. I am afraid he caught his
death the last country sessions, where he would go to see
justice done to a poor widow woman and her fatherless

Promoting. Urging the adoption of.
You was. A common seventeenth-century use with the
singular *you.*
Country. Country-side.

children, that had been wronged by a neighbouring
gentleman; for you know, Sir, my good master was
always the poor man's friend. Upon his coming home,
the first complaint he made was, that he had lost his
roast-beef stomach, not being able to touch a sirloin,
which was served up according to custom; and you
know he used to take great delight in it. From that time
forward he grew worse and worse, but still kept a good
heart to the last. Indeed we were once in great hope
of his recovery, upon a kind message that was sent
him from the Widow Lady whom he had made love
to the forty last years of his life; but this only proved
a lightning before death. He has bequeathed to this
lady, as a token of his love, a great pearl necklace,
and a couple of silver bracelets set with jewels, which
belonged to my good old lady his mother: he has
bequeathed the fine white gelding, that he used to ride
a-hunting upon, to his chaplain, because he thought
he would be kind to him; and has left you all his books.
He has, moreover, bequeathed to the chaplain a very
pretty tenement with good lands about it. It being a
very cold day when he made his will, he left for mourning, to every man in the parish, a great frieze coat,
and to every woman a black riding-hood. It was a most
moving sight to see him take leave of his poor servants,
commending us all for our fidelity, whilst we were not
able to speak a word for weeping. As we most of us
are grown grey-headed in our dear master's service,
he has left us pensions and legacies, which we may live
very comfortably upon the remaining part of our days.
He has bequeathed a great deal more in charity, which
is not yet come to my knowledge, and it is peremptorily
said in the parish, that he has left money to build a
steeple to the church; for he was heard to say some
time ago, that if he lived two years longer, Coverley
church should have a steeple to it. The chaplain tells
everybody that he made a very good end, and never

Lightning. Last flash of life (quotation from Shakespeare).
Peremptorily. Confidently.

speaks of him without tears. He was buried according
to his own directions, among the family of the Coverleys,
on the left hand of his father Sir Arthur. The coffin
was carried by six of his tenants, and the pall held by
six of the Quorum: the whole parish followed the
corpse with heavy hearts, and in their mourning suits,
the men in frieze, and the women in riding-hoods.
Captain Sentry, my master's nephew, has taken possession of the hall-house, and the whole estate. When
my old master saw him, a little before his death, he
shook him by the hand, and wished him joy of the
estate which was falling to him, desiring him only to
make a good use of it, and to pay the several legacies,
and the gifts of charity which he told him he had left
as quit-rents upon the estate. The captain truly seems
a courteous man, though he says but little. He makes
much of those whom my master loved, and shows great
kindnesses to the old house-dog, that you know my poor
master was so fond of. It would have gone to your heart
to have heard the moans the dumb creature made on
the day of my master's death. He has never joyed
himself since; no more has any of us. It was the melan-
choliest day for the poor people that ever happened in
Worcestershire. This is all from,

> Honoured Sir,
> Your most sorrowful servant,
> EDWARD BISCUIT.

P.S.—My master desired, some weeks before he died,
that a book which comes up to you by the carrier,
should be given to Sir Andrew Freeport, in his name.

This letter, notwithstanding the poor butler's
manner of writing it, gave us such an idea of our good
old friend, that upon the reading of it there was not
a dry eye in the club. Sir Andrew opening the book,
found it to be a collection of Acts of Parliament.

Quit-rents. Charges on the estate.

There was in particular the Act of Uniformity, with some passages in it marked by Sir Roger's own hand. Sir Andrew found that they related to two or three points, which he had disputed with Sir Roger the last time he appeared at the club. Sir Andrew, who would have been merry at such an incident on another occasion, at the sight of the old man's handwriting burst into tears, and put the book into his pocket. Captain Sentry informs me, that the Knight has left rings and mourning for every one in the club.   O.